# Next Step: HOPE

························································

## The Story of Operation Walk

MY QUEST TO HEAL THE WORLD
ONE NEW JOINT AT A TIME

## LAWRENCE DORR, M.D.

**Next Step: Hope**
*The Story of Operation Walk*

© 2021, Lawrence Dorr, M.D.

OPERATION WALK

www.operationwalk.org

ISBN: 978-1-66780-4-897 (hard cover)

# TABLE OF CONTENTS

# FOREWORD:

## He'll Never Stop Inspiring Us

· · · · · · · · · · · · · · · · · · · · · · · · · · · · · · · · · · · · · · · · · · · · · · · · · · · · · ·

### BY JERI WARD, R.N.

Executive Director, Operation Walk Los Angeles

E ight months later, I still can't believe he died. Wait Dr. Dorr, we're not finished yet! In my heart I know that he would *never* think his work was finished. In my thirty-seven years of knowing him, time after time I thought he had reached the pinnacle of his career, only to see that he'd come up with yet another idea!

Operation Walk is his legacy. He is the one who inspired and challenged us to bring his dream to fruition. He nurtured it and made it grow. He used to say, "Jer, we have to stop being a mom and pop thing and grow this organization." Well, I think Mom and Pop didn't do too badly. Starting small the way we did gave us heart. The hurdles we jumped made us strong. The "mistakes" we made were really just lessons we could pass along, so the teams that developed after us didn't need to reinvent the wheel.

Losing Dr. Dorr was a sucker punch that I was not prepared for. There's still so much to do. For years he had dreamed of writing a book about Operation Walk with hopes that its story would inspire new generations and its sales would bring in funds to help us with our missions. He retired from his daily practice in June of 2019 and started working on this book. The pandemic of 2020 gave him time to focus on it, and each day bought a new call or email to me, checking facts and sharing memories of what happened so long ago.

He was a smart man, bringing his friends and colleagues into Operation Walk, ensuring that this life-changing mission will carry on. He trusted his team, which really kept us on our toes. I can remember how he always left me messages like, "Find a referral to a doctor in Timbuktu who can sew an ear on sideways on Tuesday morning," or, "Get me a helicopter to take me to…" some small town in another country that I wasn't even sure *had* helicopters—but you know something? I always figured it out. I never wanted to disappoint him.

I think that when he started Operation Walk, a lot of us wondered if we could really do what he asked of us, but for him and for Operation Walk, we all found a way. He could be a taskmaster, but it was always for the sake of creating better care for his patients. He was a gentle chin-chucker to all the ladies when he made patient rounds, a macho fist-bumper to the men. The patients adored him and thought he was God. I saw the side of him that fought hospital administrators to keep his team together, that advocated for fair access to health care, and that reveled in being a kind and loving husband and father.

Over the years, Dr. Dorr and I supported each other through the usual health maladies. Both of us were mentally tough and quick to bounce back, and when he became ill in 2020, I was sure he would "kick it" the way he always did. But this time it was not meant to be. My very first thought was "What about the book?" Was it finished? He'd put so much into it. Fortunately, he left mountains of notes and interviews, so that the writer he'd been working with, Donna Frazier Glynn, could complete this book as he intended.

It was an honor to help him with Operation Walk. He carved a broad path for all of us to follow and keep Operation Walk moving ahead. In this book, he tells the story of how Op Walk came to be, how it changed him, and how it grew. I hope it inspires you as much as he inspired us in life.

*JW*

August, 2021

# INTRODUCTION:

## The Start of Something Big

·······································································

In 1994 I fell through a hole in time that changed my understanding of medicine and carried me into the soul of healing. What I saw on a brief trip to Russia sparked an idea that transformed my sense of self, my place in my profession, and my relationship to the world. You could call it a quantum change, and it set me—and many others—on a humanitarian odyssey that became the pride of my life: Operation Walk.

I'm a hip and knee surgeon, an inventor and researcher, a teacher, and for all those reasons I'd been invited to demonstrate new techniques to surgeons at Moscow's leading orthopedic hospital.

I arrived with a small team I'd rounded up at home in L.A.—an internist, a couple of anesthesiologists, and a surgical technician—expecting to walk into a hospital and an operating room much like those at home. However, it was clear from the start we weren't in Los Angeles anymore, or even, perhaps, in the 1990s. The buses and trucks on the streets looked like the ones we'd had in the Iowa farm towns where I grew up in the '50s, and the Russians supplied us with a vintage VW bus that would only start if we gave it a push and hopped in.

We were scheduled for a 9 a.m. hip replacement, and when we arrived at the hospital we were shocked to see knee-high weeds growing along the walls and steps of the entrance. A nurse led me to an outer section of the operating room and showed me where to wash my hands, a regular sink with regular soap—no sign of the sterile brushes and Betadine antiseptic soap that we were used to. Afterward, she told me to sink my hands into a bowl of acetic acid (the active ingredient of vinegar), a traditional disinfecting process that I'd heard of but never used in all my years of practice. She set a small hourglass beside me, letting me know that I should leave my hands and forearms submerged until the all sand in the glass had filtered from top to bottom.

When I entered the O.R., the usual protocols were all askew. The scrub nurse put my gloves onto my hands but touched my bare skin, contaminating her own gloves, and when I looked at the leg being prepped for surgery, it was being washed with bare hands by a surgeon named Igor, who later boasted that the infection rate at the hospital was an imperceptible—and impossible—0.0000000001 percent. At home, I ask my anesthesiologist to set the patient's blood pressure at 80 systolic to reduce blood loss and make my operative field more visible, but when I found it set at 120 and made a request to lower it, I was told, "It is not possible." I tried asking again without any luck, so I began the operation by cutting a few small vessels and letting them bleed a bit until the blood pressure was at a working level for me. The anesthesiologist walked away to sit with his back against the wall for a nap. (One of the anesthesiologists I'd brought with me stepped in to monitor the patient.)

The operation itself went smoothly, and afterward our hosts showed us to a dining area with a long table, where we sat together for a lunch of chicken and vodka—one bottle for every four people. It was only midday, but the Russians reached for the bottles and filled their glasses as if they were pouring water, even though they'd be going back to the O.R. for more surgery that afternoon. That raised eyebrows. In the U.S. we could lose our license for drinking between cases. Sitting with the head surgeon, Yuli, and our translator, I did a double take when I heard that the Russian orthopedists typically handled just two cases a day. My usual load was eight joint replacements in an operating day.

This wasn't medicine as we knew it.

Leaving the hospital we passed a museum room that paid tribute to Konstantin Sivash, a surgeon/inventor who had operated there and worked in the 1950s and '60s to develop Russia's first artificial hip, which he presented in 1963, a few years before I graduated from medical school. The idea of removing a worn-out hip joint and putting in a mechanical replacement was gaining ground then, and people like Sivash were trying to replicate the smooth glide of cartilage in the hip socket using metal, plastic, or ceramics, and puzzling out how to attach the new parts in the body and make them stay. Sivash's one-piece design was made from titanium salvaged from out-of-commission planes, Yuli said, and it resembled a rounded shower head attached to a long metal pipe. Sivash had innovative ideas for holding the device in place, but implanted in the body, this model had been a disaster. Yuli told me that they removed every one they put in, and the museum cases were filled with failed Sivash hips.

Progress in medicine is built on failure, and the Sivash design led to a successful one in the U.S., but in Russia it was almost as though the decades of advances that followed, including widely used implants that I had developed, had never happened. In the U.S. there were multiple companies competing to sell hip and knee implants to surgeons, but Russia didn't produce a single reputable one. By 1994 total joint replacements were safe, fast, and commonplace in wealthier countries across the globe, and I had assumed that Russia, a superpower I'd learned to fear in duck-and-cover drills in the '50s, would surely be among them. However, in such a large country, doctors were doing almost no joint replacements at all. There, as far as people with crippling arthritis and deteriorating or injured knees and hips were concerned, it might as well still be 1940—or 1840—when there was no recourse but to suffer with every step.

I could see the evidence of that the next day when I worked on a complex joint replacement for a person whose knee was badly deformed. It had stiffened into a fixed 45-degree angle, bent and pointing inward. This is as difficult a knee replacement as can be done, and it told me that patients in Russia had to keep going on worn-out joints—that's what leads to this kind of deformity. I successfully reconstructed the knee with one of my own implants and even Igor, a true Communist who would not give an inch to the United States, said, "Dat vas very gut!"

# A Cosmonaut, a Midnight Train Ride, and a Big Idea

After two days in that premier Russian hospital, I couldn't wrap my head around the way basic medical practices—life-and-death essentials like sterile conditions and sobriety—were neglected, and how few of the major advances in our field were visible. If things were this bad here, how must they be in "underdeveloped" countries? I'd made it to the top of my field thinking the whole world was making the climb and feeling the benefit of our collective medical evolution. We could speedily and safely implant amazing new joints in an hour and a half now, but "we" was a much smaller group than I thought. I'd been living in a bubble, I realized, and it knocked me back to feel it burst.

All this was at the back of my mind at the end of our last day there, as Yuli's wife, Valentina Tereshkova, gave us a window into a Russia that was more like the one I'd pictured before I arrived. Valentina, a former skydiving and parachuting champion, had climbed into a space capsule at age twenty-six and become the first woman to circle the Earth on a solo mission. She took us through Star City, the cosmonaut training center, and then brought us into her home for a dinner cooked by her mother. It was a feast, with three bottles of vodka that we were now free to drink and fast-flowing stories of the multi-country tour she had taken on her return from space, complete with a look at the gifts she'd received from world leaders. The gift she was most excited about that night, though, was a box of drugstore cosmetics my wife had sent with us for her at Yuli's request. Inexpensive cosmetics my wife took for granted.

Yuli may or may not have been much of a surgeon, but Valentina, still energetic and full of charisma, was a bona fide national hero. When she drove us to catch the midnight train to St. Petersburg, she was besieged by autograph-seekers, and her celebrity secured us a spot in a deluxe first-class car. We climbed on with our translator and the bottle of Armenian cognac Valentina had given us for the road, and we drank and talked for the whole six-hour trip. It was early summer and the sun barely set in St. Petersburg, which probably contributed to our excited recapping and brainstorming, as did the high of Valentina's stories and liquor. I liked and admired Valentina, and I felt sorry that a great scientific push like the one that had put her into space hadn't elevated Russian medicine.

I had an idea.

"What if we put together a team to train surgeons in other countries?" I asked my teammates. My friend John Brodhead, the internist, nodded, so I kept going. Even if all we did was make brief trips like the one to Yuli's hospital, we could improve people's surgical techniques and make medicine better around the world!

Surprisingly, no one rolled their eyes, and we kept playing out possibilities instead of calling each other impractical or grandiose. We'd all seen how inferior the Russian team had been to doctors in the U.S. and noticed how much they'd picked up by working with us even a short while.

As we talked and drank and kicked the idea around through the night, I had the same feeling that drove me early in my career, when I was a resident at L.A. County Hospital in the 1970s. There were eight of us in my residency year, and because County served a low-income population with a hefty share of community violence, we were on call to cover a steady flow of gunshot and stab wounds, motorcycle accidents, and health conditions that had been neglected until they bled into the ER. We were usually awake for thirty-six hours at a time, and I'd had the strong sense that we were all in the foxhole, covering each other's backs, so when a junior resident with a weak work ethic went to bed when we were on call, I just did the work for both of us and never said a word. I was acutely aware that we weren't all equal as doctors, but that didn't diminish the need to help my teammates, whom I knew would return the favor.

Even this much farther down the road, I could see how much it would mean to have the backs of doctors who needed an infusion of help, the way the Russians clearly did. We'd all be better for it.

When we arrived in St. Petersburg at dawn, I picked up a local newspaper and by chance my eye fell on a story about the charitable group, Operation Smile, which travels the world doing surgery on poor children to correct cleft lips and palates. Operation Smile. Tumblers clicked in my brain. Ha! We'd call this new project of ours, whatever it was, "Operation *Walk*," and maybe we'd take our surgical skills on the road to do free knee and hip replacements in poor countries for people who couldn't get them otherwise. We could pass on what we knew to local doctors, bring safe practices with us, and mentor medical teams as we helped patients. As for those patients—however many of them there would be—before we left, we'd have them walking again.

## The World We Found

Twenty plus years later, I can tell you that improbable as it was when the alcohol and euphoria wore off, we did go home to start Operation Walk, which has grown to be an international organization that's sent hundreds of doctors around the world to do the transformative work of healing and teaching that we dreamed of that night. We had no notion then of what it would take to do that, what we would see, or how it would change us.

Just as we didn't anticipate the conditions we found in Russia, we couldn't fully imagine the sorts of patients we'd encounter in places like Managua, Nicaragua. There, every case brought us in contact with the reality of lives that had been frozen in a time that was rarely touched by the kind of care we routinely provided to patients back home. Now we saw not just ill-trained doctors and broken health systems but intense suffering that was going untreated.

From the start, there was an endless stream of patients like Escarleth Meza, who came into our Managua clinic pushing a makeshift walker fashioned from a shopping cart. She was a sturdy woman in her 40s with short black hair brushed back from her forehead and a face that was set in a determined grimace. Her bare left foot rested on the rod between the cart's back wheels and we could see that the knee of that leg was several times its normal size. It looked like a boulder perched over her shin, which was oddly set back.

She moved herself along by leaning heavily on the handles of the cart to put her weight on her hands so she could lift her good leg and jump forward. She hopped fairly quickly, but it seemed to take all the energy she had.

Escarleth told us that her knee had been injured two years earlier when a wall of her house fell down. Like many in Managua, she lived in a simple home built from cinderblocks stacked with no mortar between them. Standing in her closet-size shower one day, she could hear children playing just outside, when suddenly their games brought them too close and they crashed into her wall, bringing it down on top of her and trapping her leg. Her knee was dislocated, the supporting ligaments and muscles torn.

In the U.S., surgeons quickly would have repaired such damage and put her back on her feet, but for Escarleth that wasn't an option. Local doctors told her that they had no treatment for her beyond stitching up her cuts. She was divorced and living alone, a hard enough situation, but now she was also handicapped, an outcast. She couldn't work, couldn't marry, and from what we could see, she could hardly smile.

Her whole situation seemed almost inconceivable—the house built of blocks that children could knock down, the dislocated knee that could've meant permanent disability, the ostracism she faced, and the isolation and loneliness that now filled her days.

Yet hardships like these were painfully common. An accident, or the simple misfortune of having arthritis, could strip people of their livelihood and their place in a community. We had never seen this level of need, but with the medical skills we took almost for granted, we could restore not only people's health but their *lives*. From the first time we traveled abroad with Operation Walk, we knew that. And our mission—to offer relief—got its hooks in everyone who went.

## Pure Gifts That Heal the Healers

It's easy to say that Operation Walk appeared fully formed in a flash of lightning on the midnight train from Moscow in 1994. In fact, I like to tell the story that way, but it's not quite that simple. Standing here at age 79 and looking back, I see a series of inspired and sometimes serendipitous moments spread out over decades, each one revealing a seed that needed to be tended with work and care and devotion before the next could fall into the ground, producing the raw material for something much bigger. Op Walk couldn't really happen until many elements—from inspiration to science to experience to advances in surgery—were there to support it.

For instance, it probably wouldn't have happened if not for an evening in 1946, when I was a five-year-old sitting at the bottom of the steep stairway of our home in the small town of Dayton, Iowa. My dad was a Methodist minister, and that night he was hosting a medical missionary named Bishop Rocky after a church meeting, where the bishop had come to raise money for his clinic. A stocky, smiling man with white hair and shining eyes, Bishop Rocky sat in the front room with my parents telling stories of saving lives in India.

I listened, rapt, and ran upstairs to get my piggy bank from my bedroom, racing back to break open the porcelain pig and scoop up a big pile of pennies. I presented my fortune to the doctor and told him to use my money to help his patients. I'd be following him into some faraway land when I could—I was going to be a doctor, just like him.

When I went into medicine, I thought I'd fulfilled my vow, but consciously or not, I held onto the essence of that promise, the clear, sweet desire to help the people who need it the most. That's what brings most of us into the healing professions, and it's surprisingly easy to lose touch with that impulse, though for many people, as for me, that desire keeps tugging at us when we veer away. It seems that every turn of my life and career was gradually deepening my insight, instincts, and experience until I had stockpiled the resources I'd need to launch my own sort of medical mission.

In this book, I had originally planned simply to tell stories about how Operation Walk brought volunteer doctors like me together with patients around the world. It's been a powerful, even holy, experience. We've seen thousands of patients, men and women like Escarleth, and brought them ease and grace, sometimes after long years of suffering. They can walk now, support a family, have children, dance, *live*. That's the gift our medical missions are so blessed to be able to give.

But from the beginning, Operation Walk did more than that. All of us were surprised to see and experience the profound effect our trips had on the medical teams themselves. We "givers" were restored by the abundant gratitude of patients and their families, by the way they gave their uncomplaining, even joyful, effort to recovery, and by the humanity that infuses our work when love, respect, and generosity become the currency of exchange.

All of this was becoming rare in the "advanced" medical systems we all came from, and we realized immediately that we had been starved for it. In our regular practices, we often offer our skills to patients who have such easy access to the surgeries we perform that perhaps without realizing it, they tend to see us as technicians whose service they can rate on Yelp, as though restoring the function of a hip or knee is less an act of healing than a service whose worth comes from its speed and convenience and perfection.

Something essential was lost when patients, insurers, and hospitals stopped seeing doctors, nurses, and therapists as humans and healers, and many became almost blind to the value of the work that restores people's bodies and takes them out of pain. Doctors began to feel like cogs in a machine, exhausted by work that seemed only to deplete them. In orthopedics, the burnout rate is forty percent.

Fortunately, the smiles, hugs and tears of joy that flow so freely from Operation Walk patients and their families replenished us all—even people like me who didn't quite realize we needed to be refilled. All of us were hungry for more of what Op Walk showed us was possible, and word spread until there were twenty groups from four countries carrying on the mission.

## If Our Stories Give You Hope, Pass It On

Thinking about how much passion I see in our team members after long days of difficult work for which the only payment is love, made me want to tell the story of who we are and how we are able to do what we do on Operation Walk. I hope that when you hear it, it will be harder to think of your own doctor as a sort of Jiffy Lube mechanic of the human body and easier to marvel, at least a little, at the art, craft, science, and devotion required to bring these now-ordinary acts of healing into being.

I can't tell every doctor's story, so I'll stick to mine, weaving it through these pages to let you see the seeds and epiphanies, science and teamwork from which Operation Walk grew.

I'm the product of a close, religious farm clan with a strong work ethic, a small-town Iowa kid who came from near poverty but was too well-loved to know it. I played team sports to let off steam and went through school with the energy and grades of someone who always wanted to know more, be better, figure things out. That was my nature, the bent I've had since I was born. Surgery, and then orthopedics, called to me because I liked the immediate gratification of being able to repair broken bodies, and almost by accident, I wound up in the brand new field of total joint replacement, guided by a pioneer in the field.

By the time of Operation Walk, I was well known for that work. The artificial hips we implanted on our first trip, to Cuba, had evolved from a design I had sketched out on a cocktail napkin years before. I'd been a pioneer of the surgery we used, and I'd been a master teacher to many, as well as learning from many others myself. I'd had some crushing setbacks, and I'd done research into bones that changed the way people in my field came to understand them.

That's just some of the life that accumulated within me and spread through the world before there was critical mass for the "epiphany" of Op Walk. The story of Operation Walk is layered with years of personal growth, science, and learning—mine and others'—and that's what's provided us with so much to give.

I'm proud that Operation Walk has helped heal the lives of so many patients, families, and communities around the world. I'm proud, too, that we've been part of the long chain of growth in our field, which transmits its skill hand to hand, practice to practice. We've developed new working methods and insights on our trips, learning from our patients and each other, and we've carried those lessons home as a gift to our patients. Perhaps most significantly, we've given our teams a sense of what it takes to restore the soul of healing to our practice of medicine.

It still amazes me that even with all I'd seen, learned and accomplished, I needed the healing of Operation Walk as much as our patients did. I hope that telling our story will be one step toward spreading this vision, helping us all bring new imagination and compassion to the way we care for one another. My greatest hope is that when you read this book, you will feel pulled to fill a great need in the world in a way that only you can, and my wish is that when someone offers you the gift of hope or healing, you will answer with love and thanks, and find a way to pass it on.

# CHAPTER 1:

## Great Idea, But How Do You Make It Go?

.....................................................................

The angel of inspiration who dropped the name Operation Walk in my lap at the end of the Russia trip was dazzling but not detail-oriented. Once I got home, I realized that I'd essentially been handed the title of a movie and a one-line synopsis and would have to write, produce, and direct the thing myself.

It took two and a half years to get it off the ground.

The bare-bones idea I carried back from St. Petersburg was that we'd form teams of doctors and medical staff who could set up shop in hospitals and run temporary clinics where we'd perform as many total knee and hip replacement surgeries as we could in a short span of operating days—probably three, maybe four. Short-term would be a necessity because we'd be asking busy, highly paid people to take time off from work or use vacation days, as I had on the Moscow trip, and then we'd be asking them to work with us for free.

I did a little back-of-the-envelope figuring. If we took five surgeons, including me, and operated three days with three operating rooms going at a time, with all of us working flat out, the way I did at home, how many procedures could we do?

In conditions like the ones we found in Russia, I could see doing maybe seven joint replacements a day per O.R., times three rooms—twenty-one operations a day. Over three days, we might be able to do sixty procedures.

That could be wildly ambitious considering that many U.S. surgeons then were doing more like four surgeries a day, but we needed a starting point, so out of habit, I aimed high. What would it take to pull that off?

A plastic surgeon in my hospital was a leader in Operation Smile, so I met with him, hoping he could point me to some kind of template for a short-term mission like this. He was effusive about how rewarding their work with children had been, but as he went into more detail, it sunk in that the scale of cleft palate surgery was far different from what we'd be doing. Operation Smile surgeons had no large, expensive devices to implant, no femur-size bones to saw. They could travel relatively light while we'd need more of everything—staff, money, equipment, tools, supplies.

I looked around for other humanitarian organizations that might be doing something more like what we imagined, but in the mid-nineties, such groups were few. Individual doctors went on personal missions, taking trauma devices to do operations. Emergency teams went into disaster areas with supplies and Doctors Without Borders set up long-term clinics in response to medical crises of all kinds, but there didn't seem to be a playbook for our sort of brief, intensive, surgery-focused project. We'd have to puzzle it out.

By "we" I mostly mean my right and left hands at the office, Jeri Ward, who made sure my practice ran smoothly, and Mary Ellen Sieben, who kept my operating room humming. I'd been working with these women practically from the time I went into practice, and for more than a decade they had listened to my ideas for streamlining surgeries and treating patients' bodies and souls, helping me set countless new projects in motion.

In addition to her experience as an emergency room and orthopedic nurse, Jeri had worked in sterilization and as a cast technician. She has the presence of someone who can hold her own (think Roller Derby), and though she was newly out of nursing school when I met her, she stood out as one of the few nurses on the orthopedic ward who didn't seem intimidated by my questions. She'd anticipate what I wanted to know about patients as I made my rounds and always had answers at the ready. Sweet and universally liked, she also proved to be a bulldog who kept tugging at your pants until you gave in. We had the same kind of tenacity.

Jeri ran the pre-op classes I set up in the evenings to let patients know what to expect from their surgeries, and when she transferred to the emergency room, I recruited her to work with me on her days off to help with the bone research I was doing. When I moved my practice to another hospital, I asked her to come along to train staff, recruit nurses for my team and run the show in my office. She made herself indispensable as the person who saw every patient that came through the door and earned the trust of all. For years, she not only taught patients how to prepare for surgery but also visited them at home two weeks after to be sure their wounds and rehab were progressing correctly. She fielded calls from anyone with a question, managed staff issues like a diplomat, and made a point of knowing *everyone*.

Mary Ellen was from a large Irish family and had the gift of order, along with a supreme talent for seeing and anticipating needs in the O.R. and helping me set up systems to keep the process smooth and efficient. We were among the first in the country to devise a way to use two operating rooms at a time, prepping a patient in one as I was completing surgery in another. That required careful and sometimes imaginative choreography, but Mary Ellen's personality was suited to detail, logistics, and flow, and she knew my every move. She helped me identify the best scrub techs, nurses, and anesthesiologists, and we merged them into a team with me at top while she orchestrated everyone below, including the anesthesiologists.

I'd picked up the team concept from my colleague, Tom Mallory, an ex-college football player like me, who liked to describe surgeons as "surgical athletes." He believed that in surgery, as in sports, success requires preparation, execution of a game plan, adaptation if the plan isn't working, and post-game analysis. Mallory was pioneer of this approach, and he'd organized his practice so that every member of a patient's care team knew the plan, was able to make independent decisions, and was in continual communication with other team members.

That was our model, and because of it, our operation spun like a top. Jeri was our coordinator outside the O.R., and Mary Ellen was our field marshal inside. On surgery days, she was at my side morning till night.

The practice was busy, which meant all three of us were, but my Russia stories—The acetic acid! The hourglass! The vodka!—piqued their interest, and the idea of helping poor people in other countries touched their soft hearts. I asked Jeri to take on the project.

"I can still remember you coming to me and saying, 'Jer, we need to get all the supplies to treat a patient, from when they walk in the door, through surgery and recovery,'" she says. "I am totally an 'outside the O.R.' nurse, but our surgical tech, Bud Farrier, Mary Ellen, and I put our heads together and made a list." Bit by bit, they catalogued every bandage, brace, and suture used on a typical patient. It was a very long list.

Before we got too far into any detailed planning, I had cleared the idea of Operation Walk with the top boss at the University of Southern California, where my practice was based. USC's president, Stephen Sample, gave us his blessing, but he stopped short of blessing us with a large donation to fund our experiment, as I'd secretly hoped he might. Jeri began to scrounge, looking for sources that could help us round up the "soft goods" we needed for fifty or sixty patients. Over weeks and months, she called and wrote suppliers and vendors to see who might be willing to donate something.

One of the contacts pointed her to an organization called Direct Relief, located in Santa Barbara, that was a medical supply house where hospitals and clinics donate their excess, used, or unneeded equipment. We were new to the idea of providing aid abroad, but Direct Relief had been doing it since 1945, and it regularly shipped medicine and medical supplies to parts of the world hit by hurricanes, disasters, earthquakes, and famine. It seemed, as Mister Rogers would put it, that we had found the helpers.

"Bud and I drove up to Santa Barbara," Jeri says, "and the visit gave me a good view of not only the supplies, but the workings of a well-oiled machine. Direct Relief had a busy front office with many people coordinating the needs of other relief groups. Our walk through the warehouse was mind-boggling.

There was everything from beds and gurneys to medications and IV supplies. Many items we needed were there, and when the time came, we turned in a list of our 'wants.'"

We knew we could gather crutches, canes, and walkers from patients who had finished rehab, and get further donations from the companies that made them, so we had sources for a sizable number of basics. However, we were lacking a few all-important preliminaries—surgeons, implants, and a destination, which was no small thing. Those elements were my territory.

## The First Surgical Team: A Band of Brothers

From the beginning I knew that our success rested on the quality and resilience of the surgeons I could round up for that first trip, and I instinctively reached for people I could trust to jump into the unknown with me, unfazed by anything that might come up. While I had enough experience and confidence to believe I could operate under a tree if I had to, I knew that more than a few people might be hesitant to step out of the state-of-the-art environments that made our work more predictable and easier to control. I couldn't fault anyone for that. I planned to sell the trip as an adventure and a chance to do good, which it certainly would be, but given what we'd seen in Russia, I knew that an equally accurate invitation would be something like:

"How'd you like to take some time off from work to put in some exhausting days working in conditions that will be unpredictable at best and risky at worst? You'll probably be seeing patients who've been walking on worn-out joints for years, and they may have cases far more complex than you operate at home. You won't have your usual team beside you. When you're not in the OR, you'll get to relax by explaining some surgical techniques to doctors who've never seen a knee replacement and likely haven't seen a total hip replacement either. No guarantees about the quality of the food, lodgings, or political situation. We'll control as much as we can, but I can't tell you exactly what we're walking into. Not to add any pressure, but errors and complications would be pretty problematic in this situation. No one knows or trusts us yet. You'll have to be fast, calm, and clean. What do you think? Sound like fun?"

Who would be game—and capable? The first people who came to mind were a couple of old friends with whom I'd become as close as brothers when we were starting out, Ron Sandler and Bob Porter. I'd known Ron since middle school, and we'd both played football for small Iowa colleges—me for Cornell, and he for Grinnell. All three of us grew up in Des Moines and reunited our freshman year of medical school at the University of Iowa in Iowa City. Bob was my roommate in both undergraduate and medical school, and I was his best man and he was mine. We bonded for life.

When I got a full scholarship to med school at the University of Iowa, Ron was there too. During freshman year, I lived in a medical fraternity house and did dishes to pay my board, playing rugby to release pressure. That house was like a foxhole. We slept in small rooms with two sets of bunk beds, and we leaned on each other to survive. Each course felt like a separate battle in the war, and none of us had any real idea yet how the pieces would fit. We often used to joke that our classes wouldn't help us at all in our real lives as doctors. We helped each other study, cramming huge quantities of knowledge—and then understanding—into our heads.

Our temperaments took Sandler and me in seemingly opposite directions—I was drawn to academics and planned to become a heart surgeon, so I stayed on after med school to finish a master's in pharmacology. From there I did my internship at Los Angeles County Hospital, handling a steady stream of trauma cases. Later, at the height of the Vietnam War, I went straight into the Navy. Back in senior year I'd paid for my wedding with the funds from a Navy scholarship, and in return they wanted three years of my life when I graduated. Sandler, who had also deferred his military service during his school and internship years, opted for the Peace Corps in Bolivia, where he took care of volunteers and community members in La Paz.

Those service years defined us, but not in the simple soldier vs. peacemaker way I expected. At my first posting, Camp Pendleton, California, I struck up a noontime tennis game and friendship with the base commander, who wound up pushing for me to go to Florida. I received anesthesiology training there, but was never sent to war. As I got to know the Navy docs, I realized that I fit in best with the banged-up jocks who gravitated to orthopedics, and purely by chance, I found my life's work. Sandler, too, chose orthopedics as a specialty, and his time in Bolivia left him with a passion for practicing medicine in developing countries and a fluency in Spanish. He was a Samaritan at heart, a perfect fit for Operation Walk.

Bob had worked as a triage doctor during the Vietnam Tet Offensive in 1968. Like us, he was drawn to orthopedics, and he completed his residency at the University of Oregon. He had moved to Twin Falls, Idaho, where he worked as a general orthopedic surgeon, and he'd volunteered to teach trauma care for Orthopedics Overseas in Vietnam and Tanzania. He was intrepid at home too, founding a whitewater rafting company and teaching continuing medical education programs in the Idaho wilderness. The two of us had once traveled with one of my master teachers to India to assist with surgical demonstrations, and I knew Porter was cool and unflappable.

Critically, Ron and Bob had the skills to handle whatever we'd be facing and the confidence to take direction for the sake of making things run smoothly. They were team players. If Operation Walk stumbled, and I didn't discount that possibility, they'd stick with me to learn from our mistakes instead of bad-mouthing the mission. I was relieved when they both said yes.

I also wanted to be sure I had someone who spoke my language in the O.R., and Don Longjohn was a natural choice. He had done his fellowship with me, which meant that for a solid year he'd been at my side, meticulously observing, practicing, then mastering the techniques I had picked up from my mentors and refined through my career. He'd become an excellent surgeon and now was on staff with me at USC. He didn't hesitate before saying yes. Another former fellow, Kurt Possai, signed on too.

Finally, I needed a recognizable name, someone at my level of practice and prominence in orthopedics. If we were successful, then the presence of a person like that would help validate the Op Walk idea and give it exposure, and if we ran into multiple complex cases, such a surgeon could step in and help me handle them.

Merrill Ritter, a fellow Midwesterner, seemed ideal. We had both come up in the first generation of surgeons learning the art of total joint replacement, and we'd devoted our careers to pushing its evolution. We were old enough to have seen patients who'd been immobilized by pain in diseased or arthritic hips and knees, and we'd been among the first to offer a novel solution—new joints—to people brave, desperate, and hopeful enough to take a chance on surgery and implants that were still proving themselves.

Merrill had studied with a giant in the field, Sir John Charnley, the surgeon who pioneered the first workable total hip replacement, which was a pair of metal and plastic pieces designed to replace the "ball" end of the thighbone and the cup of bone it rests in at the hip. Laser-focused on how to improve his implants and the surgery to put them in place, Charnley opened a center devoted to doing just one procedure extremely well—a revolutionary move in in an era when most orthopedists were all-purpose bone doctors. Creating systems to streamline the surgery, he could do a hip replacement in one hour, as opposed to the three or even four hours it still takes some surgeons, while achieving consistent results and setting up safe operating conditions—models for patient care that still inspire the best people working today.

Merrill had come home carrying Charnley's ambitious imprint and became the first person to do total hip and knee replacements in Indiana, then built his own hip and knee surgery center, using Charnley's systems as a guide. I'd gotten to know him because both of us had made a career of advancing what our pioneering mentors had taught us. Merrill had documented the results of his surgeries and studies in hundreds of articles, and he was among the people I sought out at conferences and followed in journals to pick up ideas and better approaches for treating patients.

My own research, much like his, was focused on finding answers that were directly helpful to surgeons. I designed implants, studied bones, worked out new incisions, and new recovery patterns—practical work that made me well known to my peers. I also started up a teaching program I called the "Masters Series" to put myself and doctors around the world in contact with innovators like Merrill.

I invited master surgeons with new techniques to demonstrate them at my hospital, working on volunteer patients. We broadcast the operations live to an audience of surgeons who gathered at the Huntington Hotel in Pasadena, California, where we all had a chance to observe and ask questions. It was always a powerful experience. When you see an operation performed by a skilled surgeon, it becomes apparent that moving through a good operation is like painting a picture. It's an art, and once you watch the process unfold, you can hold the whole picture in mind and keep learning from it.

Merrill was one of the true artists, so as I was recruiting my team, I knew I wanted him—not just to help back me up, but to give the doctors we'd meet the same kind of exposure to the best in the field that he and I had gotten. I invited him to come out to give a Masters' demonstration, and afterward, as he relaxed on my living room couch, I told him about Operation Walk and asked him if he'd join us. All I could promise, I said, was that we'd have an unforgettable time—good or bad. He agreed to come and said that he'd bring a team of three or four others from Indiana.

## Supplies: Check. Surgeons: Check. Implants...

We were moving toward critical mass, but we still needed implants—and each knee or hip system (the "kit" containing the prostheses and installation hardware) cost $5,000. Having no seed money hadn't hindered us so far, but the implants we needed might cost several hundred thousand dollars, which was no small sum for an "organization" that so far had a budget of $0.

I'd learned that the price of implants was a significant factor in why patients in so many locations couldn't get surgery. In some areas, operations were done strictly on a "bring your own implant" basis, which might mean paying more than what some impoverished patients might earn in a decade, if reliable devices were even available.

On this front, however, I had a connection—a close and cordial relationship with Intermedics, an implant manufacturing company. On a fortuitous evening when my work was just becoming known, I'd sat at a table in a New

Orleans restaurant with my mentor and an Intermedics rep. As we ate and talked, I sketched out the idea for a new hip implant on a cocktail napkin, and came away with an agreement to design it. I spent many months afterward figuring out how my imagined pieces would work in the body and how to make them safer to implant. It would be a romantic end of the story to say my first attempt worked, but, unfortunately, it failed, so I learned from what went wrong and tried again.

I had long spent my evenings after work dissecting cadaver hips at my hospital and doing detailed anatomy studies to refine my understanding of the structures surrounding the hip joint, and now I sawed and measured thigh bones in my garage to develop a new curved "stem" for the implant, an anchor piece that's fitted into the femur like a sword in a sheath. I also came up with a simple way to guide surgeons away from a couple of critical nerves and blood vessels that could cause injury and debilitating pain if they were nicked or cut. That was one of the major risks of the surgery, and by carefully positioning the screw holes in one of the pieces of the implant, I reduced that risk substantially. Elements of my design became the new standard, and my implant was still on the market a decade later, finally being retired in 2013 after its long run.

The company's willingness to take a chance on me as I developed the prototype had ultimately been very lucrative for them, and we were on the best of terms. I'm not that good at asking for money, but asking Intermedics to donate a large quantity of my own implants so I could give them away was easy. Rich Cadarette, one of the company's top sales agents, loved the idea of Operation Walk and said he could probably get us as many as we needed.

## Destination: Cuba

I felt as though I'd retraced and mined my whole career, and practically my whole life, on the Op Walk scavenger hunt, and we were tantalizingly close to having a solid foundation. However, all of us were stymied when it came to the final piece that our first mission hinged on: a place to go. We couldn't just show up in some random country where we were unknown to anyone, and say, "We're here!" On that front, we weren't quite sure where to start.

Then one of my patients, Bernard "Buddy" Litten, came in for a post-surgery checkup. Buddy, who worked in retail related to travel and duty-free shops, was a talker—and an inveterate connector. When I mentioned Operation Walk, he lit up and said he had the ideal place: "Cuba!" Yes, he acknowledged, there was a trade embargo, and you couldn't travel there directly from the U.S. No, he'd never visited, but we should go because the Cubans needed help. Restrictive U.S. policies had made them hate us, so they should know that government policies notwithstanding, there were generous, humanitarian Americans too.

I was dubious. The Cubans were Communists and Fidel Castro was a dictator, and having grown up in the Cold War, I was used to labeling them the enemy. The U.S. government still did, and the last thing we needed were political complications, but Buddy persisted. Operation Walk was supposed to be about people helping people, not about governments, right? And the Cubans were suffering. He said he knew someone who would love our idea and could help us make all the arrangements we'd need. "You should talk to her," he insisted. So with no other prospects on my list at that moment, I said I would.

Buddy put us in touch with Estela Bravo, a noted documentary film-maker who grew up in Brooklyn but had lived in Cuba since 1962. She'd landed in Latin America after meeting her husband, Ernesto, at an international student conference in the 1950s, and since moving to Havana, the two of them had collaborated on scores of films focused on Cubans, the Caribbean, and Latin America. Ernesto was a biochemist who had graduated from medical school in Argentina with Che Guevara and was currently a professor at Havana University. We couldn't have gotten a more valuable introduction—Ernesto knew the Cuban medical system well and he and Estela had high-level connections to ease our way.

Estela, a compact bundle of energy with a wide smile and a Brooklyn accent, was enthusiastic about Operation Walk and flew to Los Angeles to meet us. With the squeeze U.S. trade sanctions were putting on its economy, Cuba didn't have the resources to offer joint replacements to most of the people who needed them, she told us. Wealthy Cubans went to Spain for those operations, and people with less money who qualified by virtue of their social status—mostly military officers—were operated by inexperienced surgeons using inferior implants made in Bulgaria. Our mission would be a welcome gift and she would help us make it happen.

She quietly began making introductions, intercepting trouble, and guiding us through the permissions we'd need to make the trip. The U.S. did allow humanitarian missions to travel to Cuba, but we'd need approval from the State and Treasury departments, and, because we'd be taking high-value cargo, we'd also have to get an okay from the Office of Foreign Assets Control. We learned what we'd have to do to make those requests and Jeri made more calls.

Estela located a hospital that could serve as our base and put me in touch with the head of orthopedics there, an English-speaking surgeon named Alfredo Ceballos. We were a year and a half into start-up mode, and now, finally, we could feel real movement.

I paid Ceballos' way to California for my Masters Series in April 1996 and used the occasion to get to know our future host and size up the situation we'd be getting ourselves into. He was warm and good-natured, and when he responded to our surgeries with awe, it showed me that he and his teams probably weren't very experienced. With limited access to prostheses except the awful Bulgarian model, they did very few hip replacements, Ceballos confirmed, and no total knee replacements at all. Ours would be the first in the country. One plus was that we'd be doing very few revisions—repairs or replacements of previous implants, which can be complicated. Knowing that helped us plan, as did the detailed questions Jeri and Mary Ellen peppered him with about the set-up on his end. Jeri and I came away with an outline in mind of what we'd be doing when we arrived, and knew we'd adapt as we went. It would be a ten-day trip in all: a "tourist" day to get our bearings, two days for setting up in the hospital, four or so days in the clinic to operate, plus one more day of care for post-op patients, and a couple days to re-pack cargo and ensure that all the patients were recovering as they should. In theory, it should all work out.

## Countdown

We set April 1997 as our target date and steadily chipped away at the long list of details remaining as we counted down the months. Now we juggled logistics. Jeri and Mary Ellen recruited volunteers from our hospital team, a job that was made easier now that we could use the allure of Cuba as a draw. We figured we'd need a team of twenty-five—nurses, physical therapists, physician assistants, surgical technicians, and electrical specialists—in addition to anesthesiologists, internists, and my surgeons. Spanish-speakers would be a plus and we had to get commitments as early as we could. Since we were asking everyone to use vacation time, some people would be required to secure it months, if not a year, in advance, so Mary Ellen and Jeri cajoled, enticed and pressed.

The supplies we tracked down now would have to be gathered and packed into a huge shipping container. We'd need to create, distribute and explain protocols. There were shots and accommodations to arrange, and final paperwork to complete. "What started out as a 'let's go do this' project was becoming very time-consuming," Jeri recalls, but luckily, she adds, "For me, the timing was right. My boys were off to the service and to college, my husband was at the peak of his career with See's Candies, and I had time, energy, and experience to commit."

Add another full-time job? Why not?

Finalizing the implant request with Intermedics brought home to me how much we still didn't know. Ceballos said his hospital would come up with a pool of about seventy-five potential patients whom we would screen and examine ourselves when we arrived, but all we had to go on at this stage was a general notion that the Cubans would likely be physically smaller than Americans and we'd probably need small implants. Until we arrived, we wouldn't know the condition of patients, have X-rays, or even a clear idea of how many surgeries we'd do and how they'd go, so we'd need implants in different sizes to cover a range of eventualities, and we'd be smart to take extras to allow for the unexpected.

We also slid in a request for five sets of operating instruments—one for each of the O.R.'s we planned to run, and one that could be rotated in while the others were being sterilized, so we could operate continuously each day. At $30,000 per set, that was a $150,000 expenditure in itself, on top of the perhaps $300,000 in implants. Providing those would be an enormous gift and vote of confidence in our ability to pull off an untried plan.

Many of our remaining costs would be covered by our hosts. The Cubans agreed to put us up in government-owned housing across from the hospital and supply each house with a cook who'd make breakfast. We'd get lunch at the hospital, and probably fend for ourselves in the evening. I planned to cover any expenses that came up, including flights and dinners, for our whole crew of volunteers. The money would come out of my research fund, which I'd built with royalties from my implants and savings from the practice. This was, in its way, research. Maybe when we returned we'd show people what we'd accomplished and raise money for future missions, but we hadn't *done* anything yet, and for now, this was a one-practice endeavor built from years of relationships, good will, and experience jumping into the deep end.

Somehow, I was more excited and curious than worried about how things might unravel. I had Jeri and Mary Ellen on one side, and trusted surgeon friends on the other. All of us would be there to do good and even have a good time.

What could go wrong?

# CHAPTER 2:

## Cuba, the First Mission

·············································································

There was a party atmosphere on the flight from Cancun to Havana as we strapped ourselves in on April 5, 1997. After so many months of planning, we were just an hour and eight minutes from Cuba. We were old friends and strangers and friends of friends who'd come in from L.A., Idaho, Arizona and New York to see if we could actually make Operation Walk more than a name and an endless chain of phone calls and letters. Cancun was our work-around meeting and departure point since there were no direct flights to Cuba from the U.S., and we used our airport and flight time to get a sense of each other.

Our AeroMéxico jet was noisy, and dinner was a dry sandwich of mysterious looking processed meat and a cup of syrupy juice that could've been drained from a can of fruit cocktail, but we also got our first tastes of Cuba's famous rum. Our boisterous, nervous energy bounced through the cabin, where our fellow passengers, from what we could gather, were predominantly German men on their way to tryst with Cuban women. One of them told us that a few days earlier, a bomb had gone off in a Havana hotel disco and there had been a scattering of other explosions in the city. There was no news coverage of it in the U.S., and little in Cuba, but apparently someone was trying to scare off tourists. No one had been injured, but it was unsettling.

It was a relief to get off the plane and see the familiar face of our host, Alfredo Ceballos, stepping forward from the small delegation that had come to greet us. We were ushered into a VIP lounge where we were treated like diplomats, with soldiers taking our passports for inspection while we settled into leather club chairs and sipped mojitos. They returned with paper ID's that would hang from red string around our necks, and we didn't see our passports again until the end. When mine finally came back, it had an entry stamp on a separate slip of paper, instead of in the book itself, so U.S. officials wouldn't question it when we returned home. Ceballos cheerfully filled me in on what to expect at the hospital. Patients. Many, many patients.

It was dark as we set out for our quarters. Face pressed to the bus window, I could make out that the road was narrow, the landscape scruffy and buildings sparse, but little else. The faded coastal glamor of Old Havana that everyone knew from photos was something we'd see later. At last we reached a small compound of two-story "protocol houses," simple and spare government lodgings the size of two-story American tract homes. Three were set near a central swimming pool and fireplace, and two more were just down the street. We'd bunk there, sharing rooms, and have the services of cooks who'd help out with breakfasts and dinners.

Our hosts piled all our luggage in the large living room of the house nearest the pool—the one that had glass doors opening onto the patio—and gathered us for a few welcoming speeches. Then we scattered to our rooms, each one simply outfitted with one wooden chair and a bed or two, but no TV or even a radio. This would be our haven for the duration.

In the morning we could clearly see the low-slung pink buildings of the Surgical Medical Research Center (or "CIMEQ," as it's called) across the street amid fringes of palms and tropical greenery. CIMEQ was the country's premier hospital, built ten years before by the Russians, and it tended to serve the country's elite far more than its poor. Ceballos, I learned, was a surgeon to the stars, but he promised to deliver us a diverse group of candidates for Operation Walk.

We sat around the pool and downed what we could of breakfast—another dry sandwich and cup of fruity syrup—then trooped across the street to take a look. We'd need to pick up speed and sprint through the day if we planned to begin seeing patients in just twenty-four hours.

Ceballos and his team met us at the hospital entrance and led us down a long breezeway that ended at an elevator to the three upper levels. Our base would be a second floor operating suite that had four operating rooms, three on one side with a fourth O.R. and a storage room on the other. Unlike the Russian hospital, this one had a scrub room (sans hourglass), but there was no air conditioning, and none of the sophisticated air exchange systems that helped keep our operating rooms at home sterile. Even in the relative cool of the morning, the tropical air felt thick and close. I was already beginning to sweat.

Our patients would be housed in the clean but dingy third-floor wards set up with six beds each, three on one side facing three on the other. If there were private rooms, we didn't see them.

We circled back to a large ground-floor waiting area, which was packed with the surgery candidates local doctors had sent us. We divided ourselves into four screening teams, each with an internist, an anesthesiologist and an orthopedic surgeon, and set out to identify our best candidates. In the exam rooms, surgeons gently moved joints, asked for histories, and looked for the stories the X-rays could tell. The ones charged with keeping patients alive during surgery, the anesthesiologists, used a four-level risk scale to size up how patients would handle the stresses of bleeding and anesthesia. Meanwhile, the internists, who saw that they would be without the lab tests and imaging they relied on at home, gamely dusted off their traditional skills of observing, palpating, and listening through stethoscopes to flag underlying conditions that could pose problems. We were looking for those who were most likely to have safe, successful outcomes, and worked to weed out anyone else.

## Gathered in Front of Us: Our Reasons for Coming

Our pace was steady, with each team carefully evaluating upwards of fifteen people. The patients were wary and hopeful, and most relaxed a bit when they realized someone on our team spoke Spanish. Ron Sandler and his wife Rita, who would work as his scrub nurse, were both fluent, as was our chief anesthesiologist Julio Raya, who grew up in Spain. My physician's assistant and a number of others were comfortable speakers as well. Many more carried phrase books or had picked up words like, "Where does it hurt?" at home.

One of the people I saw that morning was a pretty thirty-year-old woman who was trained as a physical therapist and had come to the clinic from the mountains of central Cuba. She was suffering from a type of inflammatory arthritis that's common in young people around the Caribbean, and her hips were so stiff that they seemed almost fused. She walked with peg legs and had to twist her body to sit.

Sandler had recommended that we replace one hip, but he called me in for a second opinion. It took only a short examination for me to understand that the woman could not abduct (spread) her legs at all, and even hygiene was a struggle for her. She wanted children, she told us, but in the mountains, there was no chance for a C-section, and with her thighs essentially locked, she could not deliver without one.

We could help her, I explained as Sandler translated, but there was no way she could achieve her goals of mobility and having children if we only replaced one hip. She tensed and a tear ran down her cheek. I asked her if intercourse was difficult, and when she nodded, I told her that unless we operated on both hips, the difficulty would persist and it would be unwise to get pregnant. I routinely did two hips at once, I added, hoping to reassure her.

She looked straight ahead, blinking back tears. Her fear was overwhelming. We were all motionless for a few moments until her husband stepped forward from the corner of the room and raised two fingers. I promised her that her prospects would be better if that's what she chose.

So much was at stake for her. She turned to me and nodded. It would be two.

As the clinic rolled on, Bud Farrier, our surgical tech, went looking for our supplies so we could set up the still bare operating suite. He came back with bad news. The cargo truck scheduled to be at the hospital "first thing in the morning" still hadn't arrived. We'd been warned that hijacking was a possibility for a high-value load like ours, so we'd had it trucked to Texas and put on a ship that would reach Havana just as we did to minimize the time it spent at the docks, but now our goods were somewhere between there and us, and no one could tell us where.

We pressed on with the exams, and at the end of the long morning, we dropped off our charts, notes and X-rays at our compound and joined Ceballos for lunch. As we finished, he asked if I wanted a cigar—of course!—and in a gesture of hospitality I won't soon forget, he sent a young doctor to the Partagás factory. Within thirty minutes, the curious among us were puffing on freshly rolled Montecristo #2 cigars. I am no aficionado, but the one Ceballos handed me remains the best cigar I've ever tasted.

Fortified, we went back to decide who would get surgery. By the time we returned, Jeri, who had seen the chaos of our files and stayed behind to impose order, had assigned each patient a number, then marked all the X-rays and charts so there could be no mistaking which X-rays belonged to which patient, and which team had screened each one. Spread out in the living room of the poolside house, our de facto conference room, we argued for and against the patients we'd seen. Some, like the woman I'd encouraged to have a double hip replacement, were young, healthy shoo-ins. Others forced us to balance the need and hope we'd seen with concerns about safety. Straightforward decisions felt weighty.

I thought about my grandfather, who'd suffered from an arthritic hip in the years before this surgery existed. When I visited him during the summer, I only saw him move from his high chair in the living room to a chair in the kitchen in the course of a long day. I always wondered why Grandpa slept sitting in his chair at night, and why Grandma always got down on the floor to slip his shoes onto his feet. That was the reality of an arthritic hip in the 1940s and '50s—the world contracted to the distance between a chair in the kitchen and one in the living room, because movement, when it was even possible, meant pain.

Here, life was even harder for many of the people we saw, and the world of a person with severe arthritis was even smaller than what my Grandpa knew. That's what we were locking these patients into if we said no, and we knew we could free them if we said yes.

We also knew that we couldn't risk complications or take a chance that someone would die in surgery, so anyone not cleared by the internist or recommended by the anesthesiologist was eliminated. We whittled our candidates to a final list of forty-six, with nine of them getting surgery on both knees or hips. Finally we had an overview of the work we'd be facing and I divvied up the cases so each surgeon would have a manageable load through the week. Merrill and I would try to take anything tricky, and Porter, Sandler, Longjohn, and Possai would assist anyone who needed help, as well as handling their own surgeries. Longjohn would take revisions and prior infections.

Practiced as we all were, we were nervous and excited about making the gears mesh in our intricate and untried machine. We went back to let the Cuban nurses know who would get surgery and who would be going home, and because patients had come from all over the country, everyone we'd chosen was checked in, whether they were scheduled for the first day or the last.

Mary Ellen and I determined the order of cases based on which surgical instruments would be available. A knee case would be followed by a hip case, for example, so there would be no wait for instruments to be sterilized, and that kind of conscious juggling would be constant so we could keep all our rooms in use. An anesthesiologist would be assigned to each O.R., and nurses and surgical techs would move as operations were completed so they could immediately assist with the next surgery on deck. We'd try to keep our familiar teams intact, but we knew we'd be improvising and finding our rhythms as we went.

## All Hands Are Equal, and All Pitch in

It was early afternoon when our cargo truck showed up, and Jeri and Bud ran to meet it. Seeing that the Cubans were in no hurry to unload our supplies, they rushed to grab boxes themselves. "We knew if we didn't get moving there would be no way we could be ready to operate the next day," Jeri remembers, "so we just kept unloading stuff and made them try to keep up with us. Then we just all started working together at our speed and things smoothed out."

The rest of our crew, doctors to dishwashers, came out to help, streaming like a line of ants between the truck and the storage room, where Mary Ellen orchestrated the placement of piles. On final check, we could account for most everything we'd carefully packed into the container, but our entire supply of morphine was gone. Jeri and the nurses had no choice but to scramble up an instant Plan B. We still had pain pills and aspirin, and we'd supplement them with old-fashioned ice packs. We could give epidurals to patients who had had two joints replaced, and for the most serious pain, we could request small amounts of morphine from the Cubans, though we knew their supplies were thin. It wasn't what we'd have done at home, but we thought we could improvise without making patients suffer.

When we finally left the hospital, we were hot, sweaty and as ready as we thought we could be, thrilled to find a bartender dispensing rum and cigars near the pool in the sultry evening, and our housekeepers grilling dinner on the barbecue. The youngest members of our crew were soon in the water and the rest collapsed in chairs. It had already been a marathon, and we were only on mile one.

## Deal-Breakers and Detente

I woke early the next morning and went with Jeri, Bud, and Mary Ellen for a final inspection of the operating room equipment. The tropical air was damp, but our surgical instruments were *wet,* a sign that the hospital's autoclaves—machines that use pressurized steam to sterilize equipment— weren't functioning properly. If instruments are wet after their heating and cooling periods, it means they are still contaminated by bacteria in the water. They're unusable.

We asked to see the machines and wound up in the hospital basement. Through our translator, I explained to the techs on duty that we wanted to be sure our instruments were sterile so they wouldn't cause infections. Bud, in his role as our surgical tech, would be in charge of the instruments flowing to our O.R.'s, and he and Lex Sensenbrenner, a biomed engineer from Operation Smile who was there to assist, stepped toward the autoclaves so they could adjust the settings. But the local staff blocked their way—and seemed to be calling security. It was some small comfort that Lex was 6'4" and had a 5th degree black belt in karate.

Soon I was face to face with a Cuban general, who ordered us to keep our hands off the machines. I explained the situation to him and he repeated his orders for us to stand down. We went back and forth like that for ten minutes that seemed to last an hour, our volume increasing with each round. It was essential that we adjust the settings, I insisted. "No," he fired back. He was in charge and he wouldn't permit our meddling. I'd been told that some Cubans were divided about our coming and there were rumors that we were there to do harm, not good. The general seemed to have heard them.

Finally, I had no choice. We couldn't operate if we couldn't trust the machines. This was a deal-breaker.

I turned to Jeri. "Pack it up," I said. "We're going home."

Fortunately, before we could leave, our friend Estela Bravo appeared from nowhere and stepped between the general and me. She'd been hovering in the hospital to help us, but I hadn't seen her that morning and had no idea she was there.

"Wait," she said.

She pulled the officer aside, speaking urgently to him in Spanish, and when the talking stopped, she had a compromise. We could alter the settings of the autoclaves, but a soldier would be stationed at each one to observe us. I smiled because no soldier would know a thing about running an autoclave.

"Thanks," I said.

We pushed back the O.R. start times to get the instruments sterilized, and then, at last, we were off.

One of my first surgeries was on a regal elderly woman who had the poise and bearing of my childhood schoolteachers. She was about five feet four with neatly coifed short, white hair, and indeed, she told me, she *had* been a teacher. At eighty-three, she seemed to have the energy of a woman in her sixties, but her knee caused her great pain, she said, and she walked with a limp. There was nothing out of the ordinary about the operation from my standpoint—she had garden-variety arthritis, nothing complicated—but we would make history. Hers would be the first total knee replacement in Cuba. A Cuban videographer had set up in the operating room, and Ceballos told me that the operation would be broadcast to a gathering of doctors in the hospital auditorium.

It took me an hour to replace her knee, and as my assistant was closing the wound, I came out of the O.R. to talk to the assembled doctors about the mechanics of what I'd done. The room had 200 seats, and I was stunned to see every one of them taken—it seemed as though Ceballos had invited all of Cuba. The video feed had been poor, but the surgeons had been able to follow the outlines of the operation and they were hungry for details.

For the next two hours, I sat on the stage with Ceballos under large photos of Fidel Castro, answering a barrage of question about how I cut the teacher's bones, balanced the joint, and positioned her implant. The doctors instinctively knew that balance was all-important to prevent biological chaos, and they wanted to know precisely how I worked toward it, detail by detail. Engrossed, excited, and eager to learn, they were as blown away as Ceballos had been at the Masters Series. It was thrilling to see. For the first time, it hit me on a gut level that we could leave a lasting mark on medicine with Operation Walk.

The operating rooms were sweltering, and Mary Ellen stayed close during the day, mopping my forehead with cool cloths. Seeing the Cubans' seemingly bottomless desire for our teaching, we accommodated as much direct observation as we could, with doctors young and old joining us in the O.R. For surgeons, the best teaching method is repetition, and this was a rare opportunity for them to see, or at least glimpse, multiple surgeries in a short period of time. To help them gain skills and take away at least one or two concrete techniques, we sat with them to explain what we were doing. Merrill Ritter stood out as a gifted teacher, even in translation, and joined me to speak in the auditorium. We each struck a pace of three to four patients each per day to create space for lectures, Q & A's, tutorials and questions.

On the floor above us, our nursing and physical therapy teams were in the wards to receive the first ordinary Cubans who'd undergone total joint replacement. All the patients were nervous, the now-bandaged ones feeling the first effects of the surgery and those with upcoming operations watching from nearby beds for clues to their fate. Our patients at home went into single or double rooms to recover, but this would be a communal experience. Family members crowded the ward, packed into the spaces between the beds, where they'd stay for the duration, carrying in meals for their loved ones, chatting and dozing, and absorbing all that went on.

Jeri worked the floor with three nurses from our home team, Vi Gabule, Linda Norris, and Marlene Keyes, gently tending patients while demonstrating how to treat wounds, change dressings, use ice and aspirin for pain, and recognize when something was wrong. They were immediately impressed by how much family members wanted to pitch in to help and how little patients complained.

Most of the Cuban nurses had been trained in the military, and they seemed leery of our nursing team at first, unsmiling and distant. "But they watched us with the first patients, then saw the great care we were giving and how we involved the families, and we made fast friends," Jeri remembers. "I think they liked our openness and confidence in our skills."

That first day, the physical therapists got every patient with a new joint out of bed to stand and take a few steps to help prevent blood clots in their veins, and though the surgical pain was still strong, many patients smiled in surprise as they put weight on their reconstructed legs. There was no question that their fresh wounds hurt, but the crippling arthritic pain some had felt day and night for years was gone—and when they realized that, they were euphoric.

Family members looked on with curiosity and wonder, and they crowded into the teaching sessions that Kyle Baldwin and Sam Ward, our physical therapists, organized to show them how to help their loved ones do simple exercises to safely mobilize their joints and how to support them in coming days when they walked down hallways and then climbed stairs. We'd never seen this level of interest before. Where families at home left nursing and physical therapy strictly to others, here they leaned in to offer care.

And patients bolstered each other. There was no privacy in the wards, but one benefit was that roommates wanted to "show off" for each other, so those with knee replacements would lift their bandaged legs off the bed to show off their good results, no matter how much it hurt. Our floor teams cheered every effort.

When our first dozen patients were all out of the O.R., the surgeons came up for rounds. The sun was low in the sky by then, and the wards were dim, but the smiles of our patients shone like bright lights. At bedside after bedside, we were met with a flood of gratitude that seemed undiminished by first-day pain. Sandler stood at the foot of one woman's bed, and when he told her he was the one who had performed her surgery, she began throwing kisses, her smile a mile wide. Ron laughed when she finally stopped and yelled, "Thank You!" in English, sealing her words with an expansive air kiss.

This was pure joy.

Gathered at the pool that night, all of us were too high on what we'd seen and done to feel our exhaustion. Starting late and walking in as strangers, we'd completed more surgeries in one day than some hospitals at home would do in several, and we'd done it using what we'd carried in ourselves, dripping in the tropical heat. Our patients didn't know yet how much we'd changed their lives, but we could tell they were beginning to feel it. Operation Walk was on its feet and striding.

And then it wasn't.

I woke the next morning to the news that in the night, someone had stolen $7,000 from the briefcase of one of the people down the hall from me, a man from a New York philanthropic group who'd come with us to observe.

A quick scan of the rest of the house revealed that I was missing my Iowa Hawkeyes cap and T-shirt, and Merrill had lost a computer. The thief hadn't made it to the rest of our quarters, as far as we could tell, but checking our storage room in the hospital, which didn't have a lock, we found that we had lost instruments and implants. We had enough equipment to continue, and we could adapt our operations to use the remaining implants, but we couldn't go on if this continued one more day.

As word of the thefts got around, the staffers at our houses were mortified and upset, and team members were rattled. I cancelled surgery for the day and arranged for a bus to take anyone not tending patients into Old Havana to see the Cuba beyond the hospital—at least the day wouldn't be a total loss for them. I spent the next tense hours with Ceballos and the general in charge of our security. Clearly, we Americans were inviting targets, and if someone had been bold enough to enter our rooms while we slept, how could I be sure that no one would be harmed? We'd heard about the disco bombing. Were we next? And what were we supposed to do if tens of thousands of dollars' worth of equipment and supplies disappeared? We couldn't make a call and have replacements delivered overnight. The morphine loss had been bad enough. This was unworkable.

There was no quick intervention to defuse the situation this time. But between my anger and Ceballos' calm diplomacy, we extracted a promise from the general that a guard would be stationed outside each of our houses, and one more at the supply room. They'd try to recover what we'd lost, he said, but we knew it was gone.

I walked the wards to boost my mood and the smiles were even broader now. Physical therapists had gotten patients onto their feet twice for a few more steps and tomorrow they'd conquer the hallways—*walking*. The ex-schoolteacher whose knee I had replaced beamed as the nurses praised the ease with which she swung her legs over the edge of the bed so she could stand. *This* operation was for all the teachers and grandmas who so rarely get to go first.

## More than Surgery—an Awakening

Our three remaining days of surgery and teaching streaked by as we found our rhythm, if not our cool. Sun streamed into huge windows in the O.R.'s and temperatures must've reached the 80s. Our sweat-soaked surgical masks stuck to our faces, making it hard to breathe. In the middle of one operation, Ritter was so hot he pulled off his gown and scrub shirt, rolled up his scrub pants, and finished the surgery with a gown over his bare chest, as the Cuban doctors did. The heat gave me incredible focus. During one of my operations, I was sweating so profusely I was driven to finish, and I had the total hip implanted in thirteen minutes. Our anesthesiologist Roberto, who was observing, exclaimed in Spanish that I was sweating pure adrenaline. He asked Mary Ellen if I was always that fast, and she joked with him that I had used a size thirteen hip stem, so I did the surgery in that number of minutes. I was sizzling in more ways than one. So was Longjohn, who took just six minutes to close the incision.

We cemented our team concept and watched it take hold. Surgeons planned operations with their anesthesiologist and O.R. room nurse. Doctors participated with the physical therapists in the post-op therapy. Our nurses taught the local nurses the treatments we used for hip and knee replacement patients. In the operating room lounge, the Op Walk doctors drew diagrams and painted verbal pictures of the operations they'd just completed so local doctors could better understand.

With every day that passed, patients seemed less fearful. Those waiting for operations saw their roommates walking, and they became confident of their own outcome. Nurses had grumbled a bit about the constant need to remove trash from the wards—the wrappers and remains of the food families were bringing in—but they were startled to come onto their shifts and also find patients already fed and bathed by their visitors. We caught on quickly that family members would be both therapist and nurse when the patient went home, and we gained confidence in them because they were genuinely involved—this was not a show. We'd been selective about building the team we brought to Cuba and now we found our support staff was much larger than we'd imagined—not just our own people, but the hospital's team, the families and the patients. In ways that we didn't experience at home, we were all in this together.

The camaraderie, willingness, and especially the continual gratitude we experienced were deeply affecting. Siblings and children, *tías* and *esposas* wept to see their loved ones' first post-op steps, and their tears of thanks spilled over to us. We were overcome by hugs and smiles, and the brave willingness of the patients to trust us and endure their first days of pain without complaint. I'd guess that ninety percent of them persevered on our regimen of ice and oral pain meds, turning away offers of morphine. They trusted that their pain was lessening and saw that every day it was easier to move freely.

I began to feel as though we were all in the midst of a kind of awakening. Patients and families suddenly realized that our promises had been real, and the whole medical team was lifted by seeing them experience what we'd done. The lame walked, and all of us felt the miracle. "I cried frequently with families and patients," Merrill Ritter said later. "Do you know what it is like to help someone with no chance of help to alleviate their pain, suffering, and immobilization? God was there with me on my decisions. I loved helping all those deserving people."

He and I and the rest of our team had jetted into Cuba with the confidence that we could fix joints. We were very good at that, and we had success—even renown—at home, but there was a hole at the center of our work, and now we knew what had gotten lost: a reverence for the gift of healing. We *all* felt that during our time in Havana. Healing wasn't a "medical transaction" or a collection of techniques. It was, as we experienced it in the crowded wards, an exchange fueled by love. It hit me as I walked down a hallway and passed the young, fearful woman whose two stiff hips I'd replaced. She was stepping carefully with her walker, her husband by her side, and she flashed a broad grin when she saw me. I learned years later that she'd had two children—her son might be the only Larry in Cuba.

Ron Sandler, whose warmth and easy Spanish brought him close to many on the wards, noticed even at the earliest stages how our work rippled out, so that operating on one person would alter the lives of many. Our patients had left home disabled, dependent, unable to work—and now they were not. A grandmother could tend the family's children. A beautiful young woman, no longer crippled, could become a mother. A once-sidelined father or grandfather could help support his family. Though we could only operate on a relative few, whole families and communities would feel the benefit, the return of life. Ron called it a multiplier effect.

On the afternoon of the fourth and final day of our forty-five-operation streak, all the patients who could come to the lobby on walkers, crutches, or wheelchairs gathered to meet those who had helped them, especially the ones who'd been busy in the operating rooms and hadn't had a chance to come into the wards. I stood in the middle of a circle of patients and team members, all of them hugging, exclaiming and smiling through tears, and thanked the patients for trusting us to operate on them.

One man picked up his crutch and held it aloft, dancing toward me with both arms raised high over his head. He stopped when he reached me, exhilarated and triumphant—a living symbol of the dream all of us had just realized.

When our celebration dispersed, Ceballos led a few of us across the street to a grassy park, where a tiny sapling stood beside a large hole. The tree was so small I didn't think it could survive, but as I lowered it into the ground, I hoped it would surprise us, the way Operation Walk had. Jeri, Mary Ellen, Dr. Ceballos and I each shoveled dirt to fill the hole and memorialize the project we'd all grown from seed.

That night the whole team filled up a restaurant where Ernest Hemingway had moored his boat. On the wall was a picture of Gilberto Fuentes, the boat's captain, who had inspired *The Old Man and the Sea*. We sat at two long picnic tables eating fish, and I sipped Hemingway's drink, Scotch with a key lime wedge. After dinner we stood up, one by one, describing what the trip meant to us. Once more, many of us wept as we recalled the faces, stories and radiant gratitude of those we'd helped. Of all the responses, the one I remember best was from Mary Ellen. "I could never have imagined that a single experience could give me a clear understanding of the glory of medicine," she said. "I have never felt this depth of meaning for what I do."

## Havana, High and Low

Though our surgery marathon was complete, we still needed to ensure that recoveries were progressing and that there was a smooth handoff to the families and hospital personnel who would monitor our patients' progress when we left. We continued to teach and lecture—and also to learn. The involvement of families in handling basic nursing and therapy chores not only took a load off our team, we noticed, it also seemed to result in loving and enthusiastic support for the patients that led to faster recovery. And there had been a kind of serendipity in the loss of our morphine on that first day. We realized as days passed that patients weren't simply being stoic about pain. They were actually getting the relief they needed from aspirin, ice, and pain pills without needing injections of opioids. We wouldn't have risked deviating from our usual protocols at home, but as we saw such strong and unexpected results, we reminded each other to consider experimenting with all these factors at home. More family help. Lighter drugs.

I jogged in the mornings to get a better sense of where I was, and what kind of lives our patients would return to when they left us. One day's run took me into Old Havana, where I stopped along a main street and looked into the window of a grocery store. The shelves were mostly empty, with products on only a couple of them and just two or three shoppers idly picking up goods and putting them back down. A worker shooed me away when he saw me, and I continued on. On block after block, buildings were dilapidated, with random windows broken and the famous pastel walls peeling and falling down. Our quarters near the hospital were plain, and our regular meals of dry sandwiches were forgettable, but at least we had steady water and power, which wasn't the case for most people in those run-down neighborhoods where families crowded into squalid apartments below lines of ragged laundry.

When I had a chance to tour more of the hospital, doctors told me it was threadbare as well. While the ratio of physicians to patients was high, there were very few supplies for treating disease. Little wonder our drugs and tools had disappeared. In the cardiology ward, it was wrenching to meet a doctor who said he had five patients and knew four of them would die because he only had medicine for one. As the hospital's situation came clear to us, the other surgeons and I changed our teaching focus. Hip and knee replacements could make a revolutionary change in people's lives, but there were no resources for surgery like that. As I first thought in Russia, we could probably make the most lasting difference by demonstrating basic techniques and best practices—clean incisions, strong anesthesia practices, sterility. Simply persuading the hospital to adopt our autoclave settings would save many lives. Our lectures turned to some of the basic "carpentry" that bone doctors could do, working with what they had.

I got another example of how difficult it was to practice medicine in a struggling country when our team went out to a seafood restaurant one evening. Our personable waiter told me he'd been trained as a doctor, and we chatted through the night. When I left him a $300 tip to thank him for his excellent service and our conversation, he told me it was more than his doctor's salary would've been for a year.

With our schedule now relaxed, I made good on my sales pitch that the Op Walk excursion would include some R&R and a chance to see Havana's fabled sights. We set aside a tourist day and I ordered up a bus to take the team on the three-hour trip to Varadero Beach, the country's premier resort. I spent that day exploring Havana with my friend Rich Cadarette, the sales rep who'd gotten us the implants from Intermedics. Rich had come to observe, but we'd made him part of our work flow and kept him busy delivering implants to surgeons—and keeping a close eye on the inventory.

Jeri rented us a car, and we chased Hemingway's legend around Havana and into his favorite bars—La Bogdeguita del Medio, home of the mojito, where every visitor signs the wall, and the Floridita, birthplace of the daquiri, where you can raise a glass to the Hemingway bust on the counter. Our most memorable stop, though, was the Partagás factory in the middle of Old Havana. From Ceballos I had learned that not all of our patients had been lucky "commoners." Some had connections—never revealed to me until later, if at all—and one of those, whom I had worked on myself, had been the wife of the minister of tobacco. That meant we were warmly received at the famous cigar factory and got the special tour.

An old woman sat in a chair with tobacco leaves piled on either side of her so she could judge each one, with the best leaves going to Cohiba Esplendidos cigars and the second best to the Montecristo No. 2. Beyond her was a room the size of a school gymnasium that was heady with the scent of tobacco. It was densely packed with dark wooden desks, where women sat rolling the leaves, their practiced fingers spinning out cigar after cigar. The guide ushered us to a small stage at the front of the room and stood at a microphone explaining that we were part of the medical team that was performing free operations for Cubans. Suddenly there was loud, rhythmic pounding as the rollers picked up their heavy, wood-handled steel knives and beat out a minute-long round of "applause." I will always remember the sound those knives made—a thunderous standing ovation.

## Powered by Full-Body Joy

Our final days rushed by, but it felt as though we'd arrived a lifetime ago. All of us were different now. The patients were walking, sitting, and yes, dancing, and our jubilant team was almost universally hungry for more. When we left L.A., I was certain Mary Ellen and Jeri saw the Cuba trip as a one-off. We'd put ourselves through so much to assemble the pieces that I couldn't see asking them to do it again, and I was sure they wouldn't be volunteering. But none of us had counted on the way serving people who needed us so much would open our hearts.

"It was so rewarding to see how much this surgery meant to them," Jeri said. "The whole experience of doing something I did not think I could do, having it be successful, meeting so many Cuban friends, spending amazing time with my colleagues and being part of something I knew would become huge—it was the happiest feeling I ever had. We helped others in the purest way. No politics, no religion, no discrimination. In two weeks, we made life-long friends and learned how to truly work together and support each other."

It seemed as though each person had their own moment when they realized that what we were doing on Operation Walk wasn't like the medicine we practiced at home. It might've been when they felt a patient's spontaneous embrace, or saw the excitement on the face of a surgeon learning a new incision, or watched a daughter reach tearfully for a mother who had been crippled with pain and now was getting out of bed or rising easily from a chair. In that moment, joy fills your body—or at least it filled mine. I always think of the gospel song sung by the Gaither singers: "He touched me—He touched me and I'll never be the same."

We didn't want that joy to end.

As we flew out of Havana toward Cancun and home, Mary Ellen and Jeri looked at me and said, "We're doing this again—and again."

# CHAPTER 3:

## China, Yin and Yang

·······························································································

The excitement of the Cuba trip only seemed to build as we returned, turning every member of the team into an ambassador for Operation Walk. Any one of us could close our eyes and be right back in Havana with families and patients embracing us or an ecstatic man holding up his crutches to dance, and our colleagues all over the hospital and community wanted to hear our stories. Nurses in the operating room and on the patient floors, and even housekeepers on the elevators stopped us to ask about how many operations we'd done, what we'd seen, and where we planned to go next. Person after person wanted to join us.

We weren't clear about our next destination though, and eager as we were to go out again, we let ourselves wait until the next right place announced itself. Planning for Cuba had been all-consuming, and as the adrenaline rush of the work and near disasters subsided after our return, we could feel what the effort cost. We wanted to bask a while in our colleagues' esteem and excitement for us. It made returning to the hectic pace of the practice a little easier.

But even in the lull that followed our re-entry, Operation Walk kept stirring. Merrill Ritter, who'd been such a key part of the team, told me that he'd found his life's mission: he was going to assemble his own Operation Walk in Indiana and set out again. "How can you not be touched by the face of a grateful patient who never thought they would ever be well?" he wrote me later.

How could we stop now, knowing what Cuba had taught us?

I admit that I thought of it a little less poetically than Merrill did. To me, the high of traveling abroad to help those grateful patients was kind of like eating potato chips: "Bet you can't eat just one!"

We could've scheduled another Cuba trip almost instantly—we'd worked out more than a few kinks in our operation there, and a logical next step would've been to build on our experience and make things easier on ourselves. We kept in touch with Ceballos to track our outcomes and knew we had left only goodwill behind, with no complications, physical or political. No one had felt threatened by our teaching or viewed us as condescending ugly Americans. We'd be welcomed back warmly anytime we wanted to go, but I held onto my original vision of teaching and operating and improving medicine around the world. For better or worse, I had a hard time thinking small, and Cuba alone felt small to me. The world wasn't besieging us with requests, though, so we bided our time until we could see a path in front of us. We knew we would absolutely need an insider to guide us, make introductions and ease our way into a new culture, wherever we went.

In my mind, cooperation from our hosts was especially important at this stage so that any mistakes we made wouldn't be announced to the world. The idea of starting another new mission gave me the same anxiety I had as a kid when my parents sent me to work on the family farms. I wasn't afraid of the physical work, but I didn't have confidence in how my uncles were assessing what I did. I wanted them to like me, and I thought they might send me home if I made mistakes because I was in an unfamiliar environment. Taking our fledgling Op Walk to a new country, I wanted to be sure that we'd be in friendly surroundings because failure among friends would not result in widespread rumors and undermine our future. I knew we'd keep learning as we went, and I wanted to safely iron out the kinks.

It wasn't so surprising, then, that our next trip, an ambitious leap to China, came at the urging of a close member of our team, Zhinian Wan, who had described Op Walk to his mentor in Beijing and gotten us an invitation to go.

Zhinian was a young Chinese orthopedist who had spent a year with me on a fellowship and proved to be so indispensable that I asked him to stay on. Seven years in, he was the star I'd expected him to be. He wasn't allowed to see patients or operate in the U.S. because he'd gotten his medical degree in China, so he became my research assistant, overseeing the fellows who collected our data and helping me analyze our results. Starting in 1990 (and continuing for the next three decades) I published more papers on hip and knee replacement than anyone west of the Mississippi, and Zhinian's name was beside mine on much of that work from 1991 forward. Not only was he brilliant, he had a work ethic just like mine.

Zhinian had just one regret about the way his career had turned out. His mentor, Dr. Lao, the orthopedics chief who had trained him at Beijing Friendship Hospital, had expected him to return and eventually be his successor. But Zhinian couldn't, not after he and his wife realized that if they stayed in the U.S. they would be free to have more than the one child allowed in China. The Wans had two children now, including a U.S.-born son named Larry, and considered America to be their home. Things had worked out beautifully for Zhinian, personally and professionally, and if we took Op Walk to Beijing, it would close the circle, and repay a lingering sense of obligation. He'd have a chance to show his peers how well he'd fared and take a victory lap that would reflect well on Dr. Lao.

China had a population of more than 1 billion, but it did very few total joint replacements in 1998. The Chinese had developed fascinating innovations, like implants with a pearl coating on their surfaces for smoother motion, but nothing close to the state-of-the-art devices and surgical techniques we'd be using. An Op Walk visit would be a chance to introduce Chinese surgeons to the many advances that had come from our work and research. That would be a coup for Zhinian and by extension, for Dr. Lao, and it was a gift I was happy to offer.

Taking Op Walk to China would be many times more complex for us than going someplace closer and more familiar, but to be honest, we didn't think much about the cultural contrast and added logistical hurdles we'd be facing in round two of Operation Walk. We just wanted to make the trip for Zhinian, and for the Chinese patients and doctors we'd be able to help and teach. The emotional high that lofted us back from Cuba made us think we could do anything anywhere.

I had no great knowledge of China, but my father, who'd wanted to be a missionary, had talked a lot about the country when I was growing up. When I was in fifth grade, he invited a Chinese exchange student from the University of Iowa to our Thanksgiving table, and later on, when the United Nations became one of Dad's obsessions, he often spoke of how a Christian medical doctor named Sun Yat-sen had helped wrest control of the country from the Qing Dynasty to found modern China, and how the nation deserved a place at the UN. Those stories unexpectedly flooded back when I applied to medical school. At my admissions interview, the professor screening me got to the end of his list of questions, leaned his desk chair back, and folded his hands to ask, "So what do you think about China being put on the Security Council of the United Nations?"

The question came from so far out in left field it threw me for a second, but Dad had prepared me well to answer. "Of course China should be included," I said, telling the professor exactly why. He was clearly pleased with my knowledge and conclusion. We met on a Friday, and the following Monday I had a letter in my box admitting me to the University of Iowa's medical school with a full tuition scholarship. I guessed that China had helped seal the deal.

Now I'd finally make it to Beijing—to offer the kind of service that had been so important to Dad. If he were looking down from above, there's no doubt he would've been smiling.

## This Might Be Expensive

The reality of China's distance from L.A.—a twelve-hour flight that can stretch to twenty-one hours with layovers—began to set in as we penciled out costs and logistics. I'd been able to cover expenses for the twenty-five people we took to Cuba, but this time we were looking at a budget that would be at least $100,000 higher, even given the same level of donated staff time, supplies, medicines and equipment. So the China leg of Operation Walk would require fundraising—a whole new venture for us.

We were still running things out of our own offices at USC—Jeri, Mary Ellen, Bud and me—and now we'd given ourselves another circus ring to manage. As Zhinian and Dr. Lau worked out approvals, introductions and preliminary communications with Chinese officials and Friendship Hospital, Jeri organized a "gala dinner" to explain Operation Walk to the community and drum up contributions.

Keeping with our low-key, seat-of-the-pants approach to Op Walk, we decided to forgo renting a ballroom and approached the Tenet organization, which owned the USC hospital, to see if we could set up a tent for an evening on the front lawn. They were happy to accommodate us since my practice was highly visible and lucrative for them, and they were eager to be associated with our humanitarian work.

I had the idea of inviting Robert Mondavi, the most famous winemaker in the U.S., to be our celebrity honoree for the evening, and when I told him about Operation Walk, he stepped up to help without hesitation. I'd replaced both of his knees and he'd been an enthusiastic fan of our practice ever since. A consummate host and charismatic storyteller, Mondavi charmed our audience of 150 friends, family, and associates with tales of helping turn Napa Valley into a premier wine region, but what brought down the house was his quip, "After my knee replacements, my sex life has never been better." Wishing the same joy to people across the world, he toasted our China venture and helped us draw enough donations that night to fund the trip. He also provided the evening's wine—and continued to fill our cups at every Operation Walk fundraiser for the rest of his life.

The spirit of Op Walk spread through the crowd as we ate and laughed and shared our Cuba stories, and we came away with a core of financial backers and Op Walk enthusiasts who loved our mission and went home with the glow that comes from giving what you can to help improve people's lives. A number of groups and organizations bought tables that night to support us, but notably missing from the list was the orthopedics department at USC. That surprised me, given the enthusiasm of Tenet and our peers when we returned from Cuba, but I was too busy to brood about it. We had a trip to plan.

We all worked nonstop in my regular practice, but Jeri, Mary Ellen and Bud found new reserves of energy for Op-Walk, once again collecting supplies, forming a team (no problems there—everyone now wanted to go), and handling logistics. The Tenet USC hospital once again donated medicines, bandages, and soft goods, and as before, the patients in our practice gave us the crutches, walkers, and canes they no longer needed. Implants came to us courtesy of Sulzer, the manufacturer that had bought Intermedics, and our old friend Rich Cadarette agreed to control the implants and accompany us to China to manage them.

With those tent poles in place, Jeri, Bud, and Zhinian made an April visit to Beijing to scout the hospital and map out our ten-day mission, which we set for October 1998.

## 'Michael Jordan' and the Forbidden City

Beijing was a world away from Havana in more ways than one. It had been impossible to miss the poverty in Cuba, where anywhere we stopped we were surrounded by rusted-out cars, buildings with peeling paint and swarms of kids asking for handouts. But Beijing was a boom town. The skies were filled with construction cranes and the streets flowed with throngs of bicycles and motorbikes—thousands of them. Jeri told me she was so intimidated by the mass of humanity streaking past that at one point she waved down a group of pedestrians and grabbed someone's arm to help her cross the street. She said it was like wading into a stampede of horses, only instead of dust, the air was thick with smog, and the Chinese wore surgical masks instead of bandanas. It was a city in nonstop motion, and its trajectory appeared to be UP.

Friendship Hospital was a modern-looking facility with equipment comparable to what we had at home, but there were surprises that reminded the scouting team why they needed to be there checking things out in person. Toilets, for example. Like those all over the country, almost all the ones at the hospital were built for squatting—not sitting—and they were so low they were essentially holes in the ground. For our team, that would simply be a cultural difference to get used to, but for patients with recent hip operations, having to squat would be a major hurdle during recovery. Zhinian said that some people might be going home to buildings where ten families shared one toilet, and there might not be running water nearby to clean their hands, so Jeri added portable commodes to our packing list, making a note that we'd need to reinforce our teaching on sanitation and hand-washing so wounds wouldn't be infected when dressings were changed.

Jeri and Bud took careful note of the hospital's sterilization equipment— we didn't want a reprise of our Cuba problems—and mapped out the distance from the sterilization area to the O.R. They also looked at the distance from the O.R. to the wards, and pressed all the buttons of every elevator to see if all the cars stopped on every floor. Cuba had taught us to assume nothing and track as much of the minutiae as we could. When you're choreographing the dance of getting people in and out of surgery efficiently, that travel time uses precious minutes.

One of the team's major discoveries was that we would have access to just two operating rooms, so instead of three surgical teams, we'd only take a couple. We thought we'd still be able to do fifty joint replacements on upwards of forty patients, but even with all our advance intelligence, we didn't know what we didn't know, and a large piece of that had to do with invisible, almost intangible elements of Op Walk: experience, expectations, assumptions, and culture. At least for me, there would be a gulf to cross.

In tourist areas like the Forbidden City, Mao's Tomb, and Tiananmen Square, Jeri and Bud drew curiosity and friendly attention. Jeri is nearly six feet tall and blonde, and she towered over the Chinese women, drawing looks and stares. Bud was a rare black man on the streets. In Tiananmen Square, the two of them were mobbed by people wanting to take their photos because they were such an unusual sight. Everywhere Bud went, there were shouts of "Michael! Michael!" from people who were sure that this good-looking American with Michael Jordan cheekbones had to be the man himself, even if he wasn't close to the right height.

Inside the hospital, though, Jeri noticed a cautious reserve from the medical staff that could come across as coldness. The smiles that had come so readily in Cuba from Ceballos and his team rarely broke through on the faces of the Chinese doctors and nurses as they kept their eyes on Zhinian's American friends. Zhinian helped thaw the atmosphere, lighting up as he chatted with old colleagues, but there was a high level of wariness. From the expressions on the faces that greeted Jeri and Bud, no one seemed happy about the upcoming surgery. I think we knew that we'd have to let our work speak for itself and expect that trust, and maybe a smile or two, would come later. In the meantime, Zhinian did his best to warm up the experience for our scouts with an insider's tour of his home turf.

"I think Dr. Wan had fun parading us around," Jeri told me. "He gave us an early exposure to *real* Chinese food. When he asked me if I wanted to eat fish, and the waiter climbed a ladder over a giant fish tank with a club in his hand, I thought, 'JW, you are *not* in Kansas anymore!'"

By the time the team left, they'd booked us into a Hyatt-like hotel (no Cuba-style bunking here!) near Wangfujing Street, an area that's been a shopping district since the Ming Dynasty. Exploring the area would be a treat for the Op Walk team once our work was done, and the location was practical—just a twenty minute bus ride from the hospital. Zhinian's restaurant excursions yielded a menu of places we could use for group meals, and the team booked those too. Mission No. 2 felt real now—we just had to nail down a few more things: staffing, supplies, shipping, travel reservations, implants and the rest of the endless details filling the endless lists that preoccupied Jeri, Mary Ellen, and Bud. I left logistics to them when they returned. I was busy in my practice and I trusted Jeri to have everything scoped out. I would work with whatever I found when I got there.

## Day One: Dead Man on a Plane

After Cuba, we could've made Rule One of Operation Walk "Plan for the unexpected." And sure enough, the unexpected was there to greet us from the first moment of the Beijing trip. On a flight carrying part of our team, a Chinese man sitting near Jeri stopped breathing, and she rushed to him to perform CPR, with help from Bud and one of our surgeons, Ron Carn, a former fellow of mine. After several minutes, it was clear they wouldn't be able to revive him and the man was pronounced dead. If they'd been closer to L.A., the pilot might've turned the plane around, but they were halfway to China, so the flight continued on its way.

Bud and Jeri helped a flight attendant wrap the body in a blanket, and midway through, the man's wife became hysterical and lunged in to tear at her dead husband's clothing. She ripped open the lining of his jacket and snatched a money belt hidden inside, then secured jewelry that had been sewn into the hem of his pants. Once she had the valuables, she calmed down and settled back in her seat, showing no further emotion. Jeri and the others re-wrapped the body and carried it to the back of the plane, where they folded it into the refrigerator of the galley.

It was Shakespearean-like tragedy mixed with what almost felt like comedy, and if it was an omen, it didn't seem like an especially promising one. But maybe we'd gotten the drama out of the way early.

I was optimistic when I saw Friendship Hospital. It was a tall building, well-furnished inside. Conditions were much better than in Cuba—air conditioning in the operating rooms was a big step up—but the emotional reserve of the patients was jarring to me. The fear Jeri and Mary Ellen had noticed in their faces looked to me like a genuine suspicion of Americans, and particularly, Western medicine. These were people who were accustomed to being treated by holistic practitioners using herbs and acupuncture. It reminded me of the way people in the U.S. had once believed in patent medicine elixirs and thought that God decided how one healed. It was only the national polio vaccine trials in the 1950s that shook loose those old ways and let many, many people see the power of science and find a new faith in modern medicine.

Almost a half century later, we'd once again be attempting to sow faith in Western medical advances—at least among those who could put aside their suspicion and distrust of U.S. doctors and come for treatment. Despite Zhinian and Dr. Lao's confidence that we'd have a full operating roster, recruiting had been difficult, and getting the recruits to follow through was even harder. The Friendship Hospital team had found us 50 potential patients, but on our two clinic days, half of them didn't show up and of the remaining group, we accepted just nineteen people and wound up replacing twenty-four joints.

I'm still not sure where those patients came from. When I talked to Zhinian beforehand, I'd emphasized that our mission was to help poor people, and he had nodded enthusiastically. However, I suspect that some of the people we selected may have been the privileged friends or relatives of someone who understood what we could do and pulled strings to get them in. We could identify patients better as we became experienced, but on our first trips, we were a bit like a newcomer on the block being pickpocketed by the wily old veteran. It would've been easy for local officials to send anyone they chose. Still, we could see from our examinations that every person we helped *needed* our help and we were grateful that they let us show who we were and what we could do. We'd have to do a lot of showing in China, because our other means of communication were taking time to break the ice.

We prided ourselves on our personal touch and I've built my practice around treating patients like members of my own family, but that put us out of step with the Chinese doctors, whose manner tended to be brusque. To my eye, the doctor-patient relationship seemed parental, with a "doctor knows best" attitude that offered little human comfort. I hoped to provide more warmth, but it wasn't easy for me to connect with the people who came into the clinic. All the patients were dressed in identical pajamas with wide blue and white stripes that reminded me of old-time prison outfits, and without seeing them in their street clothes, I had few clues about their station in life. No one spoke unless spoken to, and the answers that came through Zhinian or one of the nurses who were translating were brief and unrevealing. Which patient was a shopkeeper or a grandmother or a clerk? What sorts of lives did they lead? What did they hope to do once their pain was gone? I had no idea and I missed being able to make that personal contact and build trust early on.

It's human nature to get suspicious if someone you don't know acts unexpectedly nice, and those first Chinese patients had their guard way up. The patients in Havana had been apprehensive about what would happen to them, but they'd been effusive about how lucky they were to be chosen for their operations. The patients in Beijing stoically held in their hopes and fears, and they rarely offered either a complaint or a thank you. Maybe they thought there would be retaliation if they got close to Americans like us. We couldn't have chosen a more dramatic cultural contrast if we'd tried, but we were there to learn as well as to help, and this was definitely a learning opportunity.

## Stepping Toward Trust

We were ever aware of being strangers in a strange land. As Jeri and Bud corralled our team to unload our cargo, our Chinese peers initially looked at us like we must be crazy—why would professionals like us—surgeons even—be carrying in boxes and piling them to the ceiling, doing the grunt work? But from day one, we emphasized that we work as a team. All of us. My wife Marilyn, who'd come as a volunteer, "washed dishes," rinsing surgical tools before they went in for sterilization. What counted wasn't our title or status, it was our willingness to contribute.

My fellow surgeons soon learned how heavily I relied on my team as we cared for patients. I needed the physical therapists to come to me and say, "I suggest we do X with this patient," and I counted on the nurses to report on patients and make suggestions about their care. People working with us picked up our rhythms and got an immediate sense of the autonomy everyone had, as well as the efficiency it gave us.

Not everyone is suited for every task though. When Jeri decided to lend a hand while we were setting up the operating rooms, she asked Rosanna Springer, one of our regular O.R. nurses from home, how she could help. Rosanna gave her a pack of sterile supplies to open—simple, until Jeri turned it upside down and the supplies tumbled out onto the Mayo stand, contaminating everything. Rosanna was horrified and I pointed my finger at Jeri to say, "You're fired!" That ended Jeri's O.R. career, which was just as well, because she already had more than enough full-time jobs.

With so few patients, our surgery schedule felt light. We did six or so joints a day in each of our two operating rooms on October 29th and 30th, staffing them with our anesthesiologists, Julio Raya and Robin Chorn, as well as two additional orthopedic surgeons, Ron Carn and Don Longjohn, and me. John Brodhead returned as our internist.

It was the anesthesiologists who had the most to contend with on this trip. Though we had planned to use spinal blocks because shots give us the most control in an unfamiliar setting, we had to revert to general anesthesia with the Chinese patients because no one trusted us enough to accept a needle in the back. That meant we had to find out in real time how reliable the hospital's anesthesia machines were. It didn't take long. On the morning of our first operations, Jeri walked into one of the O.R.'s and found one of our nurses falling asleep in a chair, with a second struggling to stay awake. An assistant at the surgical table had fallen asleep holding retractors. This wasn't jet lag. One of the anesthesia machines was leaking enough gas to put the whole surgical team under. We repaired the leak—and reinforced our resolve to use only spinal blocks and epidurals on our next trips.

I was glad to have Zhinian assisting as I worked. Chinese residents scrubbed in with us, and as in Cuba, we also had curious students and surgeons in the room watching. Zhinian translated for me and answered questions. He was the big man on campus during our stay because of his proximity to me, and especially because he knew our research inside out. We were doing what would be some of our most significant work in that period, studying how patients fared with implants that weren't held in place with cement, testing new metal-on-metal implants, and looking at how we might use bone grafts in the revision surgeries we do when implants need to be replaced. The Chinese doctors were knowledgeable about general orthopedics, but because they had little experience with joint replacement, they were intensely curious about what we were learning.

We had a lot of time for explanations and we made the most of it. We did X-ray sessions with the doctors to show them what we looked for when patients had arthritis and explained how what they saw in the X-rays could prepare them for what they'd find in surgery. We also introduced them to my method of using X-rays to categorize the bone tissue in the femur to determine what kind implant procedure would be most suitable. They were impressed to meet the Dorr behind the "Dorr bone types" study that had come on the scene just five years before and was on its way to being one of the most cited studies in orthopedic journals.

All this would be something to build on if our Chinese peers ever had a chance to begin performing total joint replacement surgery. We just had to hope that the exposure we were able to offer would create enough excitement to entice them to try.

On the wards, our physical therapists, Jennifer Lundberg and Beth Habelow, held classes for the therapists they'd be leaving in charge of the patients and worked with the floor nurses as well. Jeri and Mary Ellen had all our orders for patient care translated into Chinese so we could leave them behind with instructions for everything from teaching patients how to wash their skin and prepare their homes to make them safe after surgery, to how to navigate stairs. As in Cuba, we showed family members how to help with physical therapy, how to change dressings, and how to spot signs of complications. There was less of a carnival atmosphere here—family members came during visiting hours and there was no one setting up camp at patients' bedsides. However, over the five days we were there, we saw the same sense of relief and surprise that had filled the wards in Cuba spread through the wards in China. It was more restrained, but it was there. By the end of our stay, our stoic patients had warmed up and there were lots of tears and hugs. We'd broken through the fear.

I didn't feel nearly as much emotional intensity as I had on the first mission, but one patient stood out clearly in my mind after we left—a woman who'd been terrified of the surgery and distraught as it approached. Our lead nurse, Lynne Zawacki, stayed with her through surgery, creating a close connection, and the woman cried to see her go when our team went home.

After we finished our surgeries, our Chinese counterparts had a grand dinner for us in the ballroom of a nearby hotel. They may have been short with their patients, but they were warm and impeccable hosts for us. We sat under crepe streamers at tables decorated with floral arrangements and covered with unfamiliar delicacies. I had to smile as Marilyn stared at a sampling of hors d'oeuvres arranged on skewers that radiated from the center of a platter, uncertain of what to take. Every skewer featured some variety of cooked insects—fried grasshoppers, scorpions, silk worm larvae—and the room was loud with the sound of people crunching through the shells. As the guest of honor, I wanted to be polite, so I gamely grabbed some grasshoppers, which weren't nearly as distasteful as I'd expected.

The remainder of the banquet was full of feasting, comradeship and toasts to a shared future.

## The Real Impact? It Came Later.

On November 1, the team spent the morning packing the cargo and tending to the patients, who were slowly walking up and down the halls now, leaning on walkers but moving without the familiar pain of their arthritis or injury. It was a new beginning.

For lunch that day, Zhinian took Marilyn, me, and Rich Cadarette to his favorite restaurant. The chef himself came to greet us and he and Zhinian decided to give us a meal to remember. The chef went to the kitchen and returned carrying a basket with a large white snake curled up inside. That would be our entrée. Marilyn hated snakes and lost her appetite. I cringed, but when the dish was served, it turned out that snake—at least that variety—tastes very much like chicken.

We joined the team on a bus and toured the Forbidden City, Tiananmen Square, and the Great Wall. It's tempting to think that if you travel as far as China, you should pack in as much work as possible and leave recreation for later, but this was people's vacation time and we couldn't let ourselves go halfway around the world without seeing where we were. Once again, Bud got the star treatment at Tiananmen Square, where he was mobbed by people asking for his Michael Jordan autograph.

An unanticipated high point for at least some of the crew came during walks through the shopping area near the hotel. It was the height of the Beanie Baby craze in the U.S., where little bean-stuffed animals with bright red tags in their ears had become hot collectibles. They were made in China, and during that trip they were everywhere, and cheaper than in America. Mary Ellen and others had been buying the toys at home and they spotted a butterfly that they knew was hard to find. Some people stuffed their bags with hundreds of dollars' worth, thinking about the millions they'd make reselling them, but the joy was short-lived. On the flight home, someone took a close look at the tag attached to one of the toys. "Butter f," it read. Almost all the toys pulled out for inspection had the same "typo" on the tag. They were worthless knockoffs, but it was all part of the adventure.

On November 2nd, the whole team left for L.A. except for Marilyn, Rich Cadarette, Zhinian and me. Zhinian stopped in the countryside to spend time with his family before going back, and Rich, Marilyn, and I remained behind because I'd been invited to Peking Union Hospital, whose doctors wanted me to show them my hip replacement technique, explaining as I went. The surgery would be transmitted by video from the operating room so a group of Chinese surgeons could watch. As I walked through the procedure, I pictured five to ten people gathered in a small room, but after I finished the operation, my Chinese host led me to meet my audience, and to my great surprise, there were 400 surgeons crowded into a large lecture hall. They gave me a standing ovation when I entered and pleaded with me to "do it again."

What that meant, I finally realized, was that they wanted to re-run the video, with me standing onstage in front of the projection screen to describe the operation so they could hear my explanations one more time. Most of them had never seen a hip replacement before, so they were excited and curious. I gave them an encore, and when I finished, I was surrounded by surgeons who wanted my email or contact information. I handed out cards. It was 1998 and I did not yet have an email address.

An important lesson for me was that we don't always know in the moment what our impact will be or where it will come from. Not understanding Chinese culture, I'd felt a little let down by the patient response—both in numbers and emotionally—because it was so different from what we'd experienced in Cuba, but as it turned out, our trip left a gigantic footprint. That short session at Peking Union was later credited with popularizing hip-replacement surgery in China.

There was a kind of serendipity to our early missions. We were introducing total joint replacement to doctors and patients in Asia and Central America at the same time implant companies were expanding into those parts of the world. In that sense, we were a Johnny Appleseed organization, spreading new ideas, new operations and new products as we worked to relieve suffering among the poor. We became models and mentors, and we made lasting friends. When I wrote a book on hip replacement surgery (hip arthroplasty) using a small incision in the early 2000s, Dr. Lao, our host at Friendship Hospital, was the person who had it translated into Chinese.

Marilyn and I made one last stop before we flew home—Xi'an, where we saw the terracotta soldiers and marveled at the way that intricate, ambitious workmanship had lasted through time. Maybe we were building an "army" of goodwill with Operation Walk, I thought. Though it seemed fragile yet, maybe it would outlive us all.

## At Home: Changing Rules, Jealousy, and Trouble

Before we left China, I was already thinking about what we could do next with Operation Walk, and how we could do it better, but when I got home, I had to deal with a crisis in my own practice—an unexpected attack from the heads of my orthopedic department. Jeri told me that our bosses had reproached members of my team while we were away, and when I called my secretary, she sobbed as she described how the hospital planned to dock the salaries of the people who'd gone on the China trip for the days they'd been away, even though they'd covered their shifts and been cleared to use vacation time. I'd been personally denounced, she added, and an executive in the department had told her to look for another job.

Jeri, Mary Ellen and I struggled to understand what had blown up and why. I probably should've read more into it when my department didn't buy a table at our fundraising dinner, but it had never occurred to me that anyone would oppose our mission of doing good for others. We asked ourselves if we'd had ulterior motives with Op Walk, and if we were doing it to gain a false sense of being "better" than our colleagues instead of being driven by purely humanitarian reasons, but we knew ourselves, and we knew that the only motive for Operation Walk was the joy of making lives and medicine better in places where people suffered for want of what we took for granted at home.

The only conclusion I could reach was that the department chiefs and executives attacking us now were jealous of our success and the high visibility of our missions, and jealous of me, in particular. I was known worldwide for my research and inventions, and with the largest orthopedic patient practice in L.A., I was doing 700 operations a year. Because my profile was so high, it was already common for outsiders to think I was the department chair. And now with Operation Walk, my team and I were at the center of yet another conversation in our community, an exciting one about humanitarian giving. I didn't feel a sense of competition with my department chair, so I hadn't realized that there was a political dimension to the way I'd run with the Op Walk idea and, as some might've put it, overshadowed him.

I admit that I was naïve. Traditionally, the role of department chairs was to promote their doctors for the benefit of the field, the patients, and the hospital. I was where I was because I'd had the backing of chairs who'd given me the freedom and encouragement to play out my ideas in an atmosphere of trust and support, not interference. I believed and taught that the fundamentals for a surgeon are experience, instinct, and intuition, and my practice had shown me that the "art" of medicine—creating a trusting, caring relationship between the patient and the medical team—contributes mightily to the patient's healing. Aleksandr Solzhenitsyn wrote that a patient feels closer to his doctor than his father, and I came to understand that trust gave rewards to both doctor and patient.

However, ideas like trust and freedom were being pushed aside in the world of medicine, and I realized I was caught in a triangular cage. Forces on one side were concerned with power, and they were competing to rule medicine. On another side was evidence-based medicine, which had gained prominence since 1990 and now wanted to standardize and regulate the treatment decisions of doctors. The final leg of this suffocating triangle was an obsession with the money medicine brought into businesses, the money that medicine cost the government, and the money doctors earned.

I felt increasingly trapped, and I didn't like it. Business interests in medicine, and doctors who agreed with them, were taking a mechanical approach that downplayed the biological chaos of disease. They seemed to look at an operation like a hip replacement as something that could and should be as simple as following a recipe, though excellent surgery requires experience, instinct, and intuition precisely because the body so often presents unpredictable puzzles that have to be solved on the fly.

As I saw it, the new world of medicine openly discounted the morality of doctors and innovators when it required governmental or institutional oversight of every medical innovation. Evidence-based medicine had its roots in the Nuremberg Trials and was aimed at ensuring that rogue doctors didn't wantonly experiment on powerless patients, but the implicit Nazi comparison at the root of the system gave people the impression that doctors couldn't be trusted, and that began to erode the relationship between the public and their doctors.

All this came to a head in my practice because I fought against losing the freedom that had made my best work possible. Evidence-based medicine hammered home the need for review and oversight during research, while I was used to working by myself and submitting my work for peer review. Every advance in medicine until the 1990s had come through discoveries and experiments that progressed without oversight committees or lengthy investigations into failures. I had designed a groundbreaking hip stem by working with bones in my garage, alone. John Charnley, the British joint replacement pioneer, first used a plastic coating in a hip socket that failed 300 times before he found a new polyethylene that worked. Risk and failure come before success, and medicine advanced with the help of patients who accepted that risk freely, aware that even an innovation that might not help them, or that helped them only briefly, would be a step toward something better.

But autonomous research was becoming a relic. When I returned from China I learned that I was being investigated for conducting a research project in the same way I had successfully done so many in the past. I had designed a new device that used metal surfaces against metal surfaces, which I hoped would allow freer movement of the hip and lengthen the life of the implant. As we did pre-surgery patient education, Jeri described the test we were conducting, which would randomly assign the experimental device to fifty patients and give an already-approved device to fifty others so we could compare the outcomes. People had been eager to sign up.

The results for the new device were excellent, and we could see that we were probably looking at a new generation of implants, a significant improvement over the old ones. Although my study was limited to fifty devices, instead of waiting for further FDA approval, I continued to implant the experimental devices on patients who wanted to be part of the research, knowing that they could receive the benefits of advances that wouldn't be approved for another year right now.

I would never consider going outside an FDA regulation today. Strict rules are firmly entrenched. But in 1995 and '96, there was a transition period between our old freedom and the new restrictions. All of us were trying to learn the limits, and in orthopedics, there was a shrug of the shoulders in response to a violation like mine. My department chair could've given me a warning or asked me to resign, but instead he chose the nuclear option and brought in the FDA to evaluate my actions, expecting that they'd discipline me and I'd be so severely compromised, he would get my lucrative practice. The FDA knew my work and understood my position though, and after an audit of our patient charts, they simply told me not to do it again.

That should've ended things, but it didn't. The chair wanted me gone and the university's institutional research board gave me a two-year suspension from research. I understood then that innovation would be very difficult if I stayed and that we had zero support for Operation Walk there, so I knew I had to go. They made it easier by firing me, though the hospital and medical staff lobbied hard on my behalf.

The disruption, though painful, turned out to be a blessing in disguise. I easily found a new home at Good Samaritan Hospital, which gave me an enthusiastic welcome, and when I moved, my patients followed. So did Jeri, Mary Ellen, and my entire O.R. crew, plus all the floor nurses we wanted and my office staff, twenty-five people in all. Good Samaritan not only allowed me to continue my research, it supported it generously, where USC never had. My research productivity and influence in orthopedics only increased.

But there was no turning back the changes in U.S. medicine. Power increasingly rested with the government, insurance companies, and institutions like universities. Surgeons had to receive permission to follow the surgical plans they made for patients, which might be denied by an employee at the insurance company who was not a doctor. Decisions were made based on money—the cost of the service to the government or insurance company—and those decisions always decreased the amount of money the doctor earned for surgery. In 1985 I made $5,000 for a hip replacement. Twenty years later I made $1,200. Meanwhile, veterinarians charged $5,000 cash for a hip replacement in a dog! With doctors devalued, patients began to view us as hired guns rather than partners in their healing, not understanding how much of medicine is intangible, and how much depends on love, appreciation, and trust.

In the midst of this sea change in medicine and the crisis in my practice, Operation Walk became a respite not just for me, but for all of the medical personnel who participated. With our humanitarian organization, we created a vehicle that let us teach new techniques and share medical advances while maintaining the values of traditional medical practice that were disappearing at home. We trusted our skills and gave them freely, with no thought of money and no outside intervention. And as our patients healed and came to know us, they gave us their trust and appreciation. In the clash of the old and the new, Operation Walk carried the *heart* of medicine—and because of that, we would succeed.

# CHAPTER 4:

## The Contrasts of Nepal

································································

After my illusion-busting experience with USC, I was glad for a chance to spend time with my mentor, Chitranjan Singh Ranawat, reminding myself of what medicine could be at its best. Chit was my role model and one of my greatest professional inspirations. He had arrived in the U.S. from India with $6 in his wallet and bottomless drive, using his superb technical skill and creativity to turn a chance internship in New York into a prestigious fellowship that became a rocket to the top of our field. Around 1970, he had developed and implanted knee replacements in sheep, and was the first to perform a total knee replacement on a patient at the Hospital for Special Surgery in New York.

First, however, he'd had to fight his way past prejudice and low pay to even get onto the hospital's staff, despite his standout fellowship there. Once he took the place he deserved, he quickly established himself as one of the visionaries on the HSS's world-renowned team of joint replacement surgeons. It was my great good fortune that he was the person who trained me during my own fellowship at HSS, focusing my skills and ambition. He handed me the keys to my life in orthopedics, as well as a template for shaping it.

I had no idea at the time what that could mean. When I walked out of HSS on my last day in 1978, I felt sad because I was sure I had missed my chance to have an impact on total joint replacement—Chit already seemed to have done it all. *If only I had been a few years earlier,* I thought. I didn't understand how medicine evolves or how seeds planted by one generation can bear fruit in the next. Changes in medicine take an average of seventeen years to become accepted, and some ideas germinate for decades. Luckily for me, Chit raised my expectations for myself, encouraged my stamina, and put me on a path to innovation with his example, introductions, and advice.

He didn't play a direct role in birthing Operation Walk, but I can look back to a trip I took with him in 1988 and see how he was there to give me a more global vision. Chit was traveling home to India that year to teach his total joint replacement techniques and he invited my old friend, Bob Porter, and me to come along and assist. I'd been to Europe with my family once and to Germany for a medical meeting, but this was my first trip to a "developing" country. (Chit's famous comment to me when I asked him early on how to succeed was, "Be more Indian and less German," and I guess this was one more way of showing me what he meant.)

He demonstrated hip replacements for a small group of surgeons in Indore, where he'd gotten his early medical training, and drew a huge medical crowd in Mumbai for a surgical "event." A big-name Indian doctor, one of the very few in the country who did knee replacements at that time, performed the surgery, which was shown on a conference room screen while Chit stood on stage moderating questions from students and surgeons, explaining what they were seeing. He was already a rock star in his homeland and people hung on his every word.

Afterward, he took us to a party at the five-story home of a businessman who'd done well importing electronics, and at the rooftop gathering, we met some of the country's elite. I spent some of the night speaking with Rajiv Gandhi, who had been appointed prime minister in 1984, after his mother, Prime Minister Indira Gandhi, was assassinated. (Rajiv himself would be assassinated a few years later.) The evening was a celebration of Chit and the work we did, and being with him made *me* something of a hero in India too. I realized that this opportunity to travel with him as he brought his skills home was an experience few doctors would have in their lifetime, and I relished it.

The trip made me conscious of how privileged I was in my everyday life in the U.S. On our ten-day visit, we stayed in hotels with just a hole in the floor for a toilet and a shower above that hole, and we went into rickety wooden buildings where neighborhood surgeons worked in ordinary rooms equipped with little beyond operating tables. The shanty towns and poverty we witnessed everywhere were unlike anything I'd seen before, and I was suddenly aware not only of the extent of the needs in the country but also of how much suffering a trip like ours could relieve, even if we could only help a few people among millions.

Still, it's a funny thing—I don't correlate Operation Walk to India. I think I expected what I saw there in a way I never did the kinds of medical conditions I witnessed in Russia. I thought of India then as Chit's country, his territory. I was just a visitor in his kingdom. I was standing apart from it, watching, instead of being immersed.

However, I was looking through different eyes when we traveled back to that part of the world a decade later. I never would have thought to go to Nepal, but Chit had been invited to a medical conference there and asked me to speak alongside him. Nepal was one of the poorest nations in the world, with about half the population living below a poverty line set at $1 per person per day. No total joint replacements were yet being done there. Anyone wealthy enough to afford the operation, which would've cost between $5,000 and $7,000, would travel elsewhere to get it. The need we saw around us was immense, as was the eagerness for medical skills, and this time, I had the means to help. When the head of the teaching hospital in Kathmandu, Mahesh Shrivastava, approached me about bringing Operation Walk, I wanted that to be our next destination.

## "This Won't Be Easy"

Jeri wasn't so sure. I asked her to get in touch with Dr. Shrivastava and fly to Kathmandu to check out the hospital and see what it would take to set up there. "To tell you the truth," she told me afterward, "my first thought when I arrived was, 'Wow, I don't know if I can bring everybody here, because it's pretty dismal.'" The conditions would test us in ways Cuba and China hadn't, and she wasn't sure, at first, if we could do good, safe work there.

Poverty was the first thing we'd see coming into town. The rutted and potholed gravel road from the airport was lined with open-front kiosks with roll-down metal gates where people both lived and set out a variety of goods for sale—trinkets, clothing, pieces of candy, pieces of raw meat buzzing with flies that they batted away. Some had open fires on which they cooked meat to sell—roadside restaurants!—with children playing at the edge of traffic. The road was packed with old pickup trucks, cars, and bicycles, and people were riding on top of buses and piled on anything that moved. Pedestrians and cattle meandered in the roadway and forced the drivers to constantly honk their horns.

One thing that stood out was how much physical labor filled daily life. There was a lot of building going on, but unlike Beijing, with its towering cranes and heavy machinery, in Kathmandu most of the work was being done by hand. Men stood on bamboo scaffolding stacking bricks to build walls with little mortar to hold them, and women hauled the bricks, carrying staggering loads in slings made from lengths of cloth looped down their backs and tied at their foreheads. People toiled in the streets, sweeping up garbage and burning it in roadside ditches. At the edge of the city, we heard, ragpicker children sifted through the garbage dumps for anything they could sell for recycling. Luckier people got jobs in tourism as guides or hotel staff, working in shops or laboring in carpet factories or the textile trade, but luck was unevenly distributed. To have painful joint injuries or conditions that limited mobility in a setting like this was to be a burden at best, an outcast at worst.

Difficult as it would be, we realized that we would likely have to screen out the neediest of the needy. People faced potentially life-threatening infections and complications if they couldn't care for themselves or be cared for by family, so we couldn't simply pull potential patients off the street or work on those who lived in lean-tos. We would keep our focus on the working poor, those who at least had family, shelter, and basic sanitation. As medical people, we had heart and compassion, but we couldn't let emotions take over. We had to stay focused on where we could do the most good when we knew we couldn't do everything. It's something we would always have to do.

The name, "Nepal Medical College," had somehow led us to expect a modern campus—an institute—but what Jeri found there on the dusty grounds at the end of a winding road was a pair of old, white buildings, one long and low, the other two stories high, set at right angles with a dirt courtyard in between. The buildings had once housed a carpet factory, and now construction was in progress to convert the space into a hospital. There would be new wards, O.R.'s and central sterilization locations, the doctors there told her, but meanwhile, conditions were rudimentary.

We would have the use of two operating rooms, both small, stark, and without ventilation or surgical lights. Sconces on the walls gave some illumination to the dim space, but we'd have to roll in portable surgical lamps near the operating tables so we could see what we were doing. Scrub sinks and overhead pipes were rusty, and little of the set-up would pass muster in the U.S.

It would take careful planning to make a trip here work, but ultimately, we could not say no to the need, and we set our Nepal mission for January 2000, assembling a group of more than forty surgeons, anesthesiologists and internists, nurses, therapists, physician assistants, surgical technicians, electricians and volunteers.

As we did our prep work at home, Dr. Shrivastava held classes to educate our prospective patients about the surgeries they might receive, creating a pool of candidates we'd see at our screening clinic. We packed supplies for fifty-five people and planned to replace upwards of sixty joints.

## Land of the Mother Goddess

Visiting the land of Mount Everest felt like an adventure to us, and I was thrilled to be bringing Operation Walk. Flying in, I had a window seat, and as we cruised at 29,000 feet, I found myself at eye level with the top of the tallest mountain in the world. The Nepalis call it Sagarmatha, the forehead of the sky, while the Tibetans who live on the other side know it as Chomolungma, Mother Goddess of the Earth.

Twenty-four thousand feet below, in the smog-prone valley that houses Kathmandu, we boarded a rickety bus and made the bumpy ride into the center of the city, where the rutted roads abruptly turned to concrete. Nepal is more than eighty percent Hindu, and it seemed there were Hindu or Buddhist temples and shrines on every block, many painted with bright colors, commonly red, some with elaborate decorations and carvings, and lines of prayer flags strung from the roofs. Finally we turned down a short street and arrived at our home in Nepal, the Yak and Yeti, a three-story wooden luxury hotel with a lobby that reminded me of a ski chalet in Utah.

In the morning, we piled onto our bus and went to see the hospital. The air was hazy with dust and pollution, and the dirt road wound past stretches lined with open storefronts, markets, and low buildings. Every passing car and motorbike kicked up more dust. Our first view of the hospital was from the top of a hill leading to its dirt parking lot, and though Jeri had prepared me, my initial reaction was to swallow hard. "So this is the Harvard of Nepal!" a colleague remarked, eyebrow raised. At the parking lot's entrance stood a shack that reminded me of the snack stand at my golf course. That was the pharmacy. Patients had to buy their drugs there, and if they needed blood for their surgery, that's where they purchased it.

We made our way to the carpet-factory-turned-hospital, and as we got our first look at the facilities, I noticed the sink where we'd scrub our hands. Above it, rubber gloves hung across a rusty wire.

"Do you use the gloves more than once?" I asked one of the local nurses.

"Yes," she answered, "we wash the blood off the gloves and fill them with water to ensure there are no holes. If they are intact, we hang them here to be used again."

Jeri and Mary Ellen had made sure we loaded up on sterile gloves and enough antibiotics to protect patients from infection, but we knew we'd need to do a lot of teaching to convey the value of procedures that might seem wasteful to the Nepalis.

At our screening clinic the next day, we found the people who came in to be shy, humble, grateful, and very poor. Patients arrived with their families, and one son carried his father in on his back. Old men walked on legs that bowed out because of their worn-out knees and older women in sari-like skirts slowly shuffled in, everyone bundled in sweaters and jackets against the cold. Younger Nepalis were often fluent in English, which made communicating easier and gave us less of a feeling of distance than we'd had in China, and our nurses used their well-honed skill of making contact and listening to people's body language as well as their words. "The whole idea is to break down communication barriers," Jeri says. "You do it with touch, the way you hold a person's arm or hold their hand. People feel your good will and begin to trust you."

But there was hesitation here as well, the kind that comes from being asked to submit to something utterly unfamiliar and risk your body by stepping into the unknown. We scheduled fifty-five patients, but fear whittled the number to thirty-four, for whom we replaced forty-five joints.

It was hard to see so many refuse treatment for the pain we saw so clearly in their faces. But it wasn't hard to imagine how alarming it must've sounded to rural Nepalis when someone explained that for the operation, you had to go to sleep and allow a strange doctor to slice you open. Your hip would be cut free from your body, and then reconnected with a metal and plastic device that would remove your pain and limp—but in the process, someone would saw off your bone. It was little comfort to hear that this was a routine operation in the United States. Maybe that was so, but none of your family or friends or anyone in your community had had this operation and could vouch for it. There was no political apparatus vouching for it here either. You were on your own. And why should you put your life in the hands of foreigners even the Nepali doctors didn't know?

Though it was disappointing, the experience gave me a sense of community with the pioneering doctors who had discovered new treatments like vaccines and tried new elective operations for diseases like cancer. Our innovations were regarded by many with skepticism, fear, misunderstanding, and sometimes even hostility—until we proved ourselves with results even the most doubtful could see. Operation Walk did that in Nepal with the help of the thirty-four brave patients who showed up to receive care. Once they left us and returned to their communities, their neighbors could see them living without pain or a limp, and they became a point of reference, living proof that our medicine worked. On our second trip to Nepal four years later, we'd have a line of people waiting for our clinic, eager for an operation. Showing up that first time, though, took courage.

## Working With What We've Got: No Saw? Use a Chisel.

Working in Kathmandu made us conscious of how freely we use resources at home. We're very protective of exposed tissue because bone infections are difficult to heal and can cause serious complications. Sterility is paramount, and it's a given that we'll use fresh protective gear for each surgery and throw away the plastic drapes we use for each patient, creating large amounts of medical waste. We see it as a necessity. But the Nepalis were accustomed to recycling and reusing everything. Though we'd already noticed the reuse of gloves, we were stunned to see that the local nurses had retrieved all the plastic discards we had bundled for the trash, washed them and draped them over bushes in the courtyard to dry, planning to return them to the supply room. We had to explain repeatedly that even though an item didn't seem torn or damaged after just one use, the material wasn't meant to be sterilized over and over and would break down, defeating our larger goal of controlling infections. We weren't sure the message was getting through, but on a short mission like Operation Walk, all you can do is educate, and hope that your lessons take hold.

I had a learning experience of my own on that trip, one I won't soon forget. The old-fashioned name for orthopedic surgeons is "sawbones" or "carpenter," from the days when orthopedics was thought to be almost a matter of carpentry, cutting apart bones, which weren't fully understood to be living tissue, and patching them back together, or removing limbs that were beyond repair. Though the field has advanced greatly, we still rely on our saws. In total knee replacement, we need to cut away the damaged end of the tibia (shin bone) and the femur (thigh bone) so we can create a working joint by implanting smooth surfaces on the end of each bone that can glide against each other.

The geometry of the joint is critical as we rebuild it, and we use small electric power saws to make precise cuts that sculpt the bone to receive the implants. In planning for our Kathmandu trip, we packed those tools as a matter of course—but we didn't think to ask about how reliable the hospital's electricity would be. I found out the hard way. I was just beginning a bilateral (both knees) knee replacement when the power failed—and didn't flick back on. The batteries in my saw died and couldn't be recharged, so I had to improvise, using an osteotome, a chisel-like bone-cutting tool that's beveled on both sides, to prepare the bone for both knees. It's the most primitive technique possible, and few surgeons in the world have done a knee replacement without a saw, but on Operation Walk missions, it's a given that we'll encounter situations we never have at home and have to innovate on the spot to achieve success. It allows us to experience the hardships—and satisfaction—of overcoming unexpected challenges that early surgeons faced. This operation, which proceeded smoothly despite the difficulty, was particularly satisfying—not that I'd want to do it again. We made sure to double check the status of power supplies on future missions, and high on the packing list was an ample supply of batteries.

## Gifts from the Heart: The Beauty of an Apple

Amid the fear that greeted us, there were also patients who understood what we were bringing and badly wanted it. A man in his early 30s heard we were coming and sent his X-rays with someone who was traveling from Kathmandu to San Francisco and got them to us. He had a hip injury that caused avascular necrosis of the hip—the blood supply to the head of his femur had been cut off and the bone had died. When that happens, the bone collapses and cartilage shears away, making the hip joint very painful when you put weight on it, or even when you don't. It's crippling. The man was so young, many doctors wouldn't have done a hip replacement even if he'd been in the U.S.—the dominant thinking then was that because an implant was unlikely to last more than twenty years, they should just operate older patients. But twenty years without pain in the prime of life means twenty good years of working, taking care of a family, and providing for yourself. That's what this man was so desperate for, and that's what we could give him. He was extremely grateful. He got his hip fixed, went back to work, and life was good again.

We also had a dignitary on our roster, Nepal's highest judge. He stood out physically because he was a tall man, larger than most of our patients, with a white beard and a fine gray shirt. We hoped he would be our Nepal "angel" on future trips, someone who could bail us out if we had problems with customs or the local police.

I don't remember many other specific patients from that trip, but I do recall the way families came every day to bring in food, which wasn't provided by the hospital. When our floor staff noticed that not everyone was receiving what they needed, they tucked food from the hotel into their bags and carried it in so we could be sure no one went hungry. We'd seen extremely poor patients on our first two trips, but in Cuba and China, Communist governments had provided a few necessities. Here, the poor had almost nothing, yet because we'd come, almost by chance, at least a few of those who suffered the most would be able to walk and climb stairs and move through a day without pain.

Many members of our team, especially the new ones, were all business when we arrived, prepared to function the way they do at home, there to get one task briskly done and move on to the next. But within hours I could see their faces soften. They'd feel our everyday work being met with waves of stunned wonder and gratitude by people who had expected their hopes to be met by disappointment, and in this environment, professional kindness became something much larger. Their hearts cracked open. All around me I could see the truth of what Rabbi Harold Kushner so wisely said: "Our souls are not hungry for fame, comfort wealth, or power... Our souls are hungry for meaning, for the sense that we have figured out how to live so that our lives matter..."

I experienced that soul satisfaction on our first trip to Cuba and it hit me again in Nepal, where our patients were humble people who lived lives of making do, and our gifts of medicine *mattered*. What I felt as I watched people realize they could walk again was a kind of joy that filled me up and propelled me on.

As we were leaving Kathmandu, one of the families approached Jeri and our lead nurse Lynne Zawacki, and held out a gift: a single apple. "We burst out in tears," Jeri said. "Those people didn't have anything, and that apple might've been days' worth of money for their family's food." It was one of the most precious and unforgettable offerings of thanks we've ever received.

Thirty-four people now could walk and we had left behind a small foundation of teaching and trust on which everyone could build. I credit our nursing and PT staffs with much of our impact. Nurses spend twenty-four hours with a patient, and in almost all countries the surgeon isn't interested in the patient's emotional state, and doesn't even answer questions. In fact, patients are intimidated by the doctor, but when we offer a model of excellent patient care through our nurses and physical therapists, change moves through the system from the bottom up. We'd see it on our next visit—when we realized our lessons on care, sterility, and teamwork were taking hold.

We were especially pleased to see the Nepalis beginning to adopt our basic operating principle of treating every member of our team as equal, because in Kathmandu, we had bumped up against the workings of the caste system. The ladies who made lunches, washed linens, and took out the trash were members of the lower castes, and at the beginning of our stay, the Nepali nurses and doctors didn't even make eye contact with them. But we made a point of embracing everyone, emphasizing that the people who do jobs that may seem menial are crucial to helping us get our work done and the patients get better. As a matter of course, we treated those workers well, thanked them, and valued their contribution to our team, and as we did, the

Nepali medical team began to see how much we all gained, and how much more efficient all of us were, when the support staff received appreciation and respect. Nods became smiles and thanks, and on return trips, we were proud to see they'd become routine.

# Op Walk Intrigue:
# The Prisoner and the King's Assistant

Over the course of a couple of days, surgeons can learn techniques and approaches from us that might significantly improve their skills as they practice them, but they can't begin to master the complexities of total joint replacement with one exposure or two, and no one expects them to. Our own Op Walk learning curve was similar. We could walk in and make enough connections to set up a successful mission, but repeat visits to a country would show us how much we had yet to learn about the culture and politics of a place. I guess you could say Operation Walk itself, guided by the strategic hands of Jeri and Mary Ellen, needed to develop its own body of experience, instinct, and intuition as we went along, the same way surgeons do.

Our second trip to Nepal, in 2004, drove that home to us, leading us into intrigues we hadn't been aware of the first time around. It showed us, too, that our reach can extend beyond the operating room, even giving us sway in the rough and tumble realm of international diplomacy.

Right at the start of our 2004 mission, we got a reminder that we'd need to be vigilant on every trip, even if things had previously gone smoothly. We thought we were a known quantity and would somehow breeze into the country, but red tape always seems to attach itself to cargo worth hundreds of thousands of dollars, and ours got caught up in customs.

Jeri had flown in a couple of days early to ensure that we'd have everything we needed when the team arrived and discovered that our supplies, drugs, tools and implants were all under the control of a customs official who didn't want to let them go. Polite requests got no results, and everything was still in limbo as most of our team landed. Desperate and determined, Jeri rounded up Bud, Mary Ellen, and Ron Sandler, who'd joined us again for this trip, and they drove to the customs warehouses in a truck. They spotted our pallets on a loading dock, and while Jeri went around front to plead our case, the rest of the crew backed up to the dock and got busy filling the truck with our goods. As Jeri tells it, "I kind of broke the customs guy down. I was crying, saying our people were coming in that night and what were we going to do? He was starting to give in, and then, when he came out and saw the truck was already loaded, I guess he figured, 'This woman isn't going away. I better sign the paper.'" So he did.

It was a close call, but a good lesson in the strategies we'd need to fall back on to keep Op Walk's wheels turning. "In a place like Nepal, you've got to be willing to stick your neck out to get things done," Jeri said. We got pretty good at that. In the face of bureaucratic tangles, we learned the power of asking for forgiveness instead of for permission, and fortunately, no one ended up in jail. It always helped that we were there to give, not to take.

On that second trip, we were happy to find construction completed on the hospital building and an eager lineup of patients clamoring for care. We asked the doctors to select seventy potential candidates for our screening day, but we could've gotten 170. Our standard operating procedures felt a little more familiar to the local team, too. Nurses proudly showed us that they remembered how to elevate limbs after surgery, and PTs picked up where we'd left off in leading exercises.

We didn't stay long enough to absorb much more Nepali culture, though many on our team explored the local shrines, but in the aftermath of the trip, we got an astonishing look under the surface of Kathmandu life. One of the patients I'd operated had been a 75-year-old VIP, whom I saw for the first time when Dr. Shrivastava, our host, led me to a private room on the second floor of the hospital. There I met a small, healthy man who was very alert and had a very bowed knee. As we left the room, I asked Dr. Shrivastava who he was.

"The assistant to the king," Shrivastava said.

Afterward, I noted the man's name: P. N. Chaudhary. His operation was successful, and he was grateful—which would likely make him a willing and well-placed angel if we needed one on a future trip.

About a year later, back in Los Angeles, Jeri was making the rounds of patients in our waiting room, helping them feel comfortable. One was a doctor from Montana who needed a hip replacement. Jeri, who knew she could always interest patients in our humanitarian missions with Operation Walk, mentioned we had visited Nepal and was surprised to see the doctor sit forward in her chair. She had been to Kathmandu repeatedly, she told Jeri, because her son was being held there in a notorious jail. It was a desperate situation. He had been there for two years, couldn't get a hearing with the court, and saw no hope of getting out. Two U.S. senators and a couple of congressmen had made appeals for his release, but the Nepali government was preoccupied with a long civil war, and even our high-level officials couldn't get the attention of the king.

Jeri called me over to hear the story, which became ever more dramatic and alarming as the doctor gave us the details of what might be our wildest Op Walk-related tale.

The son, in his thirties, had been traveling in Tibet and had gone to Nepal to catch a flight home. He was arrested, his mother said, because he was carrying $25,000 in American currency. He'd collected the money to translate the work of Tibetan monks into English, she said, and when he refused to hand it over to the police in exchange for his freedom, they confiscated it *and* tossed him in jail. I figured that the officials thought the cash was drug money. The Nepalis have a strong intolerance for drug trafficking and are notoriously tough even on users—the penalty for possession there is twenty years in jail, while for murder it is only eleven. It made sense to me that the authorities had stonewalled the appeals from American politicians because they assumed the son had a drug connection.

It wasn't our responsibility to investigate. What we knew for sure was that the son had been thrown in jail with no charge, which meant there was no reason to schedule a court appearance, which meant he was trapped.

The mother described the jail as bleak and corrupt. There were 900 prisoners, of whom ninety-nine percent spoke only Nepali. Most were addicts who could easily get drugs inside the jail, so they slept all day. The rest milled around a central courtyard surrounded by brick walls eight feet thick and forty feet high with barbed wire strung across the top. This fortress had once been a military barracks, but now its rooms were open wards, with 120 men to a room. Prisoners slept on primitive wooden benches eighteen inches wide and six feet long, which were lined up in long rows, with two feet between one "bed" and the next. Each man had a blue water bucket, freshened twice a week, to use for cleaning up and brushing his teeth, and drinking water came from a common pump. Diarrhea was not uncommon. We feared for anyone living under those conditions.

Money ruled the prison society, our patient said. Because it was assumed that no one could break out, there were no guards inside. Instead, the warden made one prisoner the boss and let him appoint others to keep order in the place and sell goods to the inmates—food, clothing, and recreational and medicinal drugs. Discipline was enforced with threats; the boss was always someone with ties to the feared Indian mafia, and he chose underlings with family in Nepal who could be made to suffer if their relatives didn't toe the line inside the prison. Still, prisoners managed to escape. The woman's son told her about a man who had gotten free by bribing the two guards who were taking him to his court date. He went to the bathroom and the guards let two hours pass without checking. When they returned, all they found was an open window. They had to spend six months in jail as punishment, but the $2,500 each of them was paid was the equivalent of five years' pay, so the tradeoff seemed worth it.

Our patient's story got even more fantastical as it went. She told us that her son, (I'll call him Joe) had become friends with a high-profile prisoner, an English-speaking drug dealer for the Indian mafia, who came by to say goodbye on his court date. He told Joe he wouldn't be back because the mafia had paid the judge to free him. We speculated that bribery seemed like a plausible escape route for Joe. His mother could supply the money, but with no charges filed against him, no one would be ferrying Joe to court and he had no opportunity to get beyond the prison walls. He wasn't sure he would ever get out.

Joe's life in the meantime was not solitary, for better or worse. He had become friends with a celebrity criminal named Charles Sobrahj, a charming sociopath and serial killer who has been described as the Charles Manson of Southwest Asia. Part French and part Vietnamese, Sobrahj had killed unsuspecting tourists, but he was kind to Joe, and played host to him in his cell, which was tricked out with a television and all the comforts he could buy with fifteen million francs, the amount he'd been paid for the rights to a movie about his life.

We listened, incredulous, to the story, and brainstormed about how to help Joe. Jeri suggested that we contact the judge I had operated on during our first Nepal mission and ask him to help. He answered my letter sympathetically, with high praise for Operation Walk and the way we had helped his tiny country's citizens, but he could not order Joe's release—final decisions were made by the king. I wrote again, this time asking the judge to forward our letter to the king's assistant. The king should know, I said, that if the American were not released from jail, Operation Walk would never again come to Nepal.

The response was swift, and this time, it was positive:

Thursday, June 16, 2005 3:41 AM

To: Ward, Jeri

Subject: Reply from P.N. Chaudhary

Thank you very much for the letter you sent to me. Yes, I very much remember you and the Operation Walk program members who visited Nepal… I am very much thankful to Dr. Lawrence Dorr for my successful operation…

You had drawn my attention to a person (Mr. "John Doe") who has been sentenced to a jail in Nepal for certain legal irregularities… The pardon petition of ("John Doe") has already been filed in the Royal Palace. I do hope some step would likely be taken after His Majesty the King returns to Kathmandu after his foreign visit by the next week. I assure you I will do my best in this regard.

Sincerely yours,

Rt. Hon'ble Parashu Narayan Chaudhary

Chairman, Raj Parishad Standing Committee

Two weeks later, Joe came to my office to thank me. I sat in my chair and looked at his smiling face, glad that Operation Walk could accomplish what two senators and two congressmen could not. It showed me the powerful ambassadorship of doing good for others and the standing it gives us to help even more.

The truth is that everyone who came into my office had always become family to us, and by extension so did everyone we treated on Operation Walk. As time went on we would become a point of contact for a growing network of Op Walk patients, and remain in touch to continue to help them as we could (though fortunately, we never had another occasion to spring someone from prison). At the center of my vision of medicine is the conviction that caring is healing, and I've always emphasized that in my practice.

What I was about to learn as we came home from Nepal the first time was how the model of pure caring built into Operation Walk would provide solace and refuge during one of the most challenging and demoralizing periods of my career.

# CHAPTER 5:

## Letting Op Walk Heal the Surgeon

．．．．．．．．．．．．．．．．．．．．．．．．．．．．．．．．．．．．．．．．．．．．．．．．．．．．．．．．．．．．．

The early 2000s arrived with a tough stretch of bumps and lessons, stresses that ultimately made me, my practice, and Operation Walk stronger. But there was a little bit of hell to go through first.

I had glided into the new millennium feeling the hope of the Nepal mission and the growth that came with our next trip, six months later, which took us back to Cuba. Merrill Ritter, the Indiana surgeon who had been such an important part of our first Cuba mission, had made good on his promise to start a chapter of Operation Walk, and to send the new group on its way, we rounded up an L.A. team to work alongside them and provide support. We older hands could mentor the new ones—and help double Op Walk's reach. Merrill knew the surgical side of Op Walk, but he and his Hoosier team had much to learn about how to build and run a mission.

Jeri and Mary Ellen started the mentoring process months in advance, coordinating logistics for our own group while guiding their Indiana counterparts through the dance of assembling the components of a mission—from fundraisers to implants, government permissions, staffing and shipping. Surgeons, it was clear from the beginning, naturally tend to turn the nitty-gritty legwork of a mission over to their key staff people—their own do-it-all versions of Mary Ellen and Jeri—so it made sense to seek out those pivotal behind-the-scenes leaders and train them directly.

Our joint mission would take us to the Frank Pais Orthopedic Hospital in Havana, and our host would be a surgeon who had been with Castro in the mountains before the Cuban Revolution. The hospital was a couple of miles inland from CIMEQ, where we'd worked the first time, so nothing was exactly the same—except for the poverty, the lack of resources, and the heartfelt warmth of the Cuban patients, staff and medical team.

From my perspective, it felt like a routine trip, brimming not just with work but with gratitude. The Operation Walk "routine" inevitably includes twists and hitches, but I always come away renewed, not least from seeing another crop of volunteers on their first mission moving from trepidation to confidence to euphoria as they fall in step with Op Walk, and then fall in love.

Jennifer Okuno, a physical therapist and longtime member of my team at home, came with us on the trip and wrote an account that reminded me of just how disorienting and even overwhelming it can be to go from the orderly routines of our runs-like-clockwork O.R.'s at home to strange settings where "makeshift" is the state of the art.

Here's how she described her experience:

*I recall being nervous and worried about the travel, my inability to speak the language confidently, the unfamiliarity of the hospital, and the overall uncertainty of what was expected of me. The week-long mission trip included a chaotically organized screening day, then four days each filled with 14-17 simple to complex unilateral and bilateral hip and knee replacements.*

*We were thrown together as strangers and quick friendships developed over meals. We shared hugs, smiles, and knowledge with Cuban staff, Cuban patients, and family members. I fumbled through Spanish phrases that I frantically looked up in my small pocket dictionary that I kept in my fanny pack. We had a communal goal of assisting these cautiously optimistic patients to their first steps towards a mobile pain-free life…*

*Patients and family members traveled for days to get to the hospital. Family members carried our patients on their backs to transport them from one place to another. We modified commonly used items for functional needs (instead of a bedside commode, a family cut a hole in the seat of the green plastic lawn chair and strategically placed a bucket under the hole.) Our patients patiently sat for long hours in the grueling heat and humidity. All of them just wanted a chance. And this is what Operation Walk does—gives hope to those who have none and gives a chance for those who aren't afforded one.*

*I had the privilege of seeing patients take their first steps with the walker and glance over to their teary-eyed family members as they mouthed the words "no dolor," meaning "no pain" in Spanish. I didn't need my pocket dictionary as the sheer optimism and mile-wide smiles translated every bit of gratitude, hope, optimism, and joy...*

*I can never recreate the feeling that I had after going on that first Operation Walk trip. I was mentally and physically exhausted but in a good kind of way. Although I was drained, I felt fulfilled... When I speak of these trips, most think I am doing something very special. I believe it's the other way around. I cannot imagine where else I would experience this amount of humility, gratitude, warmth, and unconditional love that I have received from the people I have met along the way.*

I'm moved by all of what Jennifer says, especially by her memory of the patients' words: "*no dolor.*" No more pain. That's what we can offer, and what both patients and the medical team feel. Relief, and the hope that comes with it. For Merrill, the second Cuba experience was a confirmation that humanitarian work was something he wanted and needed to do for the rest of his medical career, and he has kept his vow to continue. Under his leadership, the Indiana chapter has been an Operation Walk anchor ever since.

## Mysterious and Agonizing Failures

The post-trip high carried me into the summer, when the first signs of trouble began popping up in my practice. I had invented an artificial hip for Sulzer Orthopedics, and I'd used it with great success from August of 1999 until April of 2000. Then I implanted one in a patient who developed severe pain six weeks or so after the operation. The device had failed.

What that means is that it had come loose in the body. The implant would have to be replaced in a second operation—a revision.

I knew the implant and the implant procedure inside out because I'd developed both of them, so I was startled by this result and focused on finding out what had happened—especially when another patient and then another had the same experience. Something had broken down, but it took many months for us to figure out precisely what it was and why it was happening.

To explain what went wrong, I'll need to say a little more about the mechanics of a hip replacement, and I'd like to take a minute to do that because I think that when we describe Operation Walk, we usually talk about patients' difficult lives before Op Walk, then show the dancing that comes after, fast-forwarding over what actually goes into the surgery itself.

It's so routine here in the U.S. that our American patients sometimes assume it's easy. I know I make it sound that way, but what our surgeons and their teams bring to Op Walk is years' worth of training and experience that allows them to do these procedures and handle the more complicated situations that come up efficiently and well in challenging and unfamiliar conditions. Their expertise is hard-won and precious, which makes it all the more remarkable to me that they freely give it away to the patients and medical personnel we meet, so let me illustrate just what they are doing. Feel free to skim this next bit if you're allergic to the marvels of science, but if you'd like a short, close-up look at what's really happening on the operating table as our Op Walk teams replace hip after hip on a mission, I think you'll be awed by what they do, sometimes in the short space of an hour, or even less.

## A New Ball and Socket

When we replace a hip, we're basically bringing back "glide" to the ball and socket joint whose cartilage has flaked away or been damaged, causing painful and destructive friction and inflammation. The ball side of the joint, the rounded top end of the thigh bone, normally has a cap of cartilage about six millimeters thick that is white, glistening, and about eight times as slippery as ice. A similar layer of cartilage lines the hip socket, and with those two slick surfaces articulating together there is little friction, but the cartilage can be injured by shear stresses, which can chip it or cause an uneven surface that then begins to fragment by peeling off slivers. (Visualize this as slivers coming off a wooden board.) When enough cartilage has worn off, the joint surface is down to bone.

Cartilage can't regrow or heal because it has no blood supply—it gets its nutrition from the joint fluid being pumped into it when the joint is compressed. And currently, we don't have a good artificial cartilage replacement, though researchers are working on a hydrogel that looks promising. In the meantime, repairing the joint means replacing the whole thing. On the ball side of the joint, we cut off the bony knob at the head of the thigh bone (femur) and replace it with a smooth metal or ceramic sphere that's held in place by a shaft that goes into the center cavity of the bone. On the socket side, we put a slick new surface on the acetabulum (pronounced assy-TAB-u-lum), the bony cup that holds the femur head. We do that by fitting in a sturdy new titanium cup that has a smooth plastic liner.

Putting the cup in correctly is the toughest surgery of all the bones for hip or knee replacement because we're working with a small structure in a big pelvis. The acetabulum is delicate, and as it's buried under muscles, it's difficult to see, so it's crucial to handle this bony structure with care. Many things can go wrong here and I spent much of my teaching time helping my fellows make it safely through this part of the procedure.

The existing bone cup is not a perfect hemisphere, but the replacement cup that will sit inside it *is*, so the bone needs to be reshaped to a hemisphere. We do this with a power reamer, which has to be directed at just the right angle. If it's aimed incorrectly, it can push through a bony wall, and a surgeon who pushes too hard can ream right through the floor of the cup. If that happens, it might take a bone graft to fill the hole. Then, when a new cup is put on top of the compromised bone, it may not stay fixed in place, and the new joint won't last.

If the surgeon reams the bone into an ellipse instead of the needed round shape, the cup might not have a good fit and it might take several screws to hold the new cup in place firmly. This too can cut the lifespan of the implant.

Many times I have taken the reamer away from a surgeon who was headed for trouble and finished this preparation myself.

It's simpler to implant the ball side of the joint, but precision is important here too. In this part of the surgery, we use a saw to cut off the head of the femur and then prepare the long shaft of bone to receive the implant's stem. With the head of the femur gone, we can see the spongy cancellous bone layer that's inside the hard outside surfaces. We cut through this spongy bone with a sharp-ended awl, then use a mallet to pound a broach, which is a piece of metal with cutting teeth, into the space inside the long bone (that space is called the intramedullary canal, or IM canal). The teeth cut a pathway for the implant stem. The position of the stem can make the leg ride higher or lower in the hip than before, and it has to be inserted carefully so the leg will be the right length and sit at the correct distance from the pelvis.

With experience, each tap and cut can be efficient. At home in the U.S. we now have the benefit of computer guidance for help with positioning the pieces, something I've helped develop so that even surgeons who are less experienced can have the kind of precision I drill into my fellows over many months. On Op Walk, of course, we are on our own, trusting our training and experience to guide us.

Once the metal cup is in place in the pelvis and stem in the femur, the surgeon taps in the plastic liner that locks into the cup, and then taps a metal or ceramic ball onto the top of the stem.

Along with all this bone shaping, pounding and positioning, there's one final element: something has to hold the new pieces in place for the long run—they have to be fixed to the bone. The hip joint rotates, so there's rotational stress pulling at the cup. The stem sitting inside the bone is under shear stresses. That's a lot of stress working to pull the implant loose, so "fixation" is crucial.

An older method of holding the implant in place to use "bone cement," which is mixed in the O.R. and changes from liquid to solid over fifteen minutes. The cement is pressurized or pushed into the spongy cancellous bone, and once it's in place, the stem or cup can be pushed into its correct position and then held there until the cement sets. When the cement is hard, the implant is secure.

Applying the cement is difficult for many surgeons because this "glue" has to enter the spongy bone to a precise depth of three millimeters to hold the implant in place. Depending on how porous the bone is, we may need to drill holes in it to allow the cement to penetrate. In the 1980s a large number of implants pulled loose because surgeons didn't have good enough cement technique, so I did extensive research to find better solutions and standardize the process. I also worked to find ways to eliminate the cement entirely.

## The Implant that Went Awry

The implant that suddenly started failing in mid-2000 reflected the best of my knowledge after a career's worth of studies and design experiments aimed at making artificial hips work, last, and function smoothly for decades. It was called the Inter-Op.

The Inter-Op was held in place with a cementless method I helped develop and refine, which had been adopted by about ninety percent of surgeons in the U.S. With non-cemented fixation, we first do something called "press fitting" to temporarily hold the cup and stem in place. We ream the acetabulum so it's a little smaller than the cup to be implanted and then pound in the implant. We might also use screws to keep it from falling out. We use a similar technique on the stem side, creating a tight opening and "press-fitting" the implant inside. Pressure braces the pieces, but what will keep them in place over time is bone growth.

It's amazing, really. The porous bone that is in intimate contact with the implant will bond to the metal pieces if we give the implant a porous surface, with pores the same size as those on the bone. The bone is "fooled" by the structure and grows into and onto it, creating a permanent attachment. Some metal implants have a rough surface instead of actual pores and that too will promote bone growth into and onto the device. This cementless fixation, as it's called, attaches the implants to the bone, and can keep them secure for thirty-five to forty years.

I was excited to be a pioneer in this fixation, and I went on to design one of the dominant hip systems using it. But now my new Inter-Op device was failing even though our studies had shown it to be a clear success.

For a time after the first failures, I kept using the implant because I thought of several causes and wanted to eliminate them. I reported the initial failures to people at Sulzer Orthopedics in July of 2000, and at the end of August, I wrote to the president of the company, telling him that seven of my patients had by then experienced the cup pulling lose from the bone and that the company should investigate. Sulzer began looking into the problem seriously in mid-September, and by mid-October I'd seen the problem in three or four additional patients. I wrote the company again, saying, "I cannot blame the Inter-Op cup because I used the Inter-Op from August 1999 until March 2000 without a single problem. Something has changed and hopefully your 'detectives' can figure it out for me."

I pulled back from using the cup, and stopped using it entirely in November. Finally, at the end of that month, an outside company hired by Sulzer pinpointed the problem. In late 1999, Sulzer had stopped using an outside contractor to manufacture the device and brought production in house. When they did, they eliminated a step in the production process. They'd been dipping the metal pieces in acid to prevent corrosion, but someone must've pointed out that because the metal was titanium, it was highly unlikely to corrode in the body. (That's why it's used in so many medical devices.) The acid bath step appeared to be unnecessary, but what no one knew then was that the acid had performed an unintended—and, as it turned out, vital—function. Traces of mineral oil could be left on the implants in the manufacturing process, and the acid bath had stripped any oil away.

When the outside investigators studied the problematic cups, they found that many of them were contaminated with a minuscule amount of oil, one-15,000th of an ounce, and that was enough to keep bone from growing into the outside surface of the implant the way it was supposed to.

Sulzer issued a recall on December 8. The contamination potentially affected 40,000 cups, 26,000 of which had already been implanted. The company estimated that of those, 12,000 risked coming loose, but the number may have been higher. Patients filed more than 1,000 lawsuits, and ultimately a large class-action suit.

## Costly Failure and a Time of Rebuilding

It was a terrible period for everyone involved, and my experience was very similar to the one faced by John Charnley, the total joint replacement pioneer. In an early design, he had used Teflon for the plastic cup, thinking it would reduce friction, but it wore terribly. Charnley did the first implants in 1959/60, and by 1961 they were failing. He wound up doing 300 revisions, and though he was working with patients who had chosen to have the new implants despite knowing they might only last a short time, he was denigrated and accused of doing human experimentation. I didn't face quite that level of criticism, but during the next year I had the same response that Charnley did: severe anxiety and depression about the failures, even though they weren't my fault.

Patients filed fifty lawsuits against me, but I was indemnified by the company so I knew I would be insulated. Still, I was consumed by the repercussions. I felt it was urgent to make things right with the people I'd operated so they'd suffer as little as possible. I personally did 125 revisions of the cups in 2001, and I received some forgiveness from patients when the company compensated each of them with $160,000 as part of the billion-dollar class-action suit against Sulzer. The company put manufacturing safeguards in place, the acid bath came back, and the company president lost his job.

Locally, my reputation as a surgeon was under attack. My peers in Los Angeles told people that my surgical technique was to blame for the failures, as did the company, at first. Like Charnley I was redeemed in the end, but it came at a price of a year of negative comments aimed at diminishing me in my own city. Surgeons in the rest of the country understood that the failures weren't my fault, and outside L.A., my honesty about what happened actually improved my reputation. However, competition for patients could be cutthroat locally, so other orthopedic surgeons told everyone to avoid me. If I hadn't had those 125 cup revisions to do, I wouldn't have had many operations in 2001.

Fortunately, we had two Operation Walk missions that year that gave me some joy and belief that all I did was not bad. They were a welcome and needed break from the anguish in my practice, but there's no question that 2001 was a difficult year all around. Even the Op Walk trip we took that January was destined to provide more challenges and lessons than relief.

By now we were veterans of four missions and felt we had gained the experience we needed to go anywhere to conduct Operation Walk. In the United States, we were no longer a startup that others were watching to see if it failed or survived. We had earned respect among those who knew about us, a small circle that continued to grow. We were hitting our stride. Beyond our annual fundraising dinner, we now had loyal donors who gave us freedom to travel. Audrey Skirball, a prominent L.A. philanthropist, donated one million dollars divided into four payments, and Chuck Miller and Jean Cohen donated $50,000-$100,000 each year. We had no paid employees so the money we raised all went to financing our trips. Now we could afford two missions a year.

## Destination: Philippines

For Operation Walk's fifth mission, we chose Cebu City, Philippines, the hometown of Vi Gabule, the total joint nurse for my practice. Vi's mention of the Philippines brought back an event from deep in my memory: my first adventure into the world outside my small town. My family had packed into the car for a ride to the big city of Des Moines, and I stared out the window the whole way, seeing only asphalt, weeds, and corn. When we arrived at our destination, I sat on an examining table while a kind doctor asked me questions. My father wanted to be a missionary in the Philippines, so the whole family had to have a medical clearance. I got the green light and so did the rest of us—except for Dad. The doctor couldn't give him a clean bill of health because he'd had tuberculosis as a boy.

Dad had been deeply disappointed, and I liked the thought that now I could be his surrogate and fulfill his dream for him, at least a little, by taking Op Walk to Cebu and serving the Filipino people, as he'd so wanted to do. Vi contacted doctors at Vincente Sotto Memorial Medical Center and we began to plan. I felt confident about going because I knew the work of Dr. Ray Gustilo, a leader in total hip and knee replacement in the U.S., who was from Manila. Gustilo, like me, was a researcher and inventor, and he too had found a calling in philanthropy. He had set up a company to manufacture low-cost implants for Pacific Rim countries, and he spent several months a year in Manila, operating and teaching local surgeons. Perhaps because he'd blazed the trail, there was strong interest in our coming to Manila, but we'd already agreed to Cebu City, so we passed on the invitation, though I agreed to stop on the way and give lectures. The surgeons knew my reputation and were eager to learn from me.

Jeri had traveled ahead to Cebu, a quick ninety-minute flight down the Philippine island chain, and been shown the operating room we'd use. However, when we arrived, there had been a switch and we were directed to an out-of-the-way spot in an outpatient facility at the back of the hospital. Much of the surgery done at the hospital was performed by medical missions, and we heard later that we had been displaced by a team performing neurosurgery. The make-do O.R.'s we wound up using were clinic exam rooms we pressed into service. They had yellow walls and were so small there was barely enough room to walk around the operating table, which had to be set at an angle to fit. With so little space, the O.R. tech had to come into the room first, then the patient, and the tech would be trapped in a corner throughout the case with no way to leave. Like the O.R.'s we'd used in Nepal, these had no permanent surgical lights, and none of the rapid-air-turnover ventilation that we thought we'd find. No air conditioning either. We were back in the Havana-like tropics, only this time we were 700 miles closer to the equator. January, it turned out, was steamy—and prone to sudden downpours.

Operating in an ordinary room with no systems to purify the air meant infection risk was high, so we used our now-familiar protocol of giving patients antibiotics for two days after surgery and leaving betadine antiseptic in the wound. Our efficiency with the operations helped too, because when an operation goes past ninety minutes, infection risk increases by twenty-five percent every twenty minutes. Fortunately, our surgeons, as always, were a focused, fast, experienced crew. We would've enjoyed having fans in the sweltering O.R., but decades earlier, John Charnley, working to reduce the infection rate in his Wrightington, England, O.R., had done air-flow tests that revealed that a wall fan was bringing in dust particles from the hallway, and each bit of dust had thousands of bacteria riding into the room with it. Air currents flowing up from the floor would deliver 50,000 bacteria a minute into the air from the body of the surgeon and from each assistant at the table. It stuck in my mind that fans were trouble, so no fans for us.

The biggest surprise in Cebu was the reception we received. For reasons that weren't quite clear, the staff and doctors didn't seem too interested in why we were there, and may even have resented our presence. While the surgeons in Manila had clamored for us to come, here, we were unknown quantities, and suspicion of us seemed high. We expected a full clinic, but the Cebu doctors made only a small number of patients available to us, and we operated just thirteen, replacing eighteen joints. We'd come a long way to help so few people, and while we thought we could use our time well to teach, I don't recall any of the local doctors joining us in our clinic or operating room. It would be the first and last time in all the years of Operation Walk that I felt we were unwanted. I've since come to realize that every team is not a match for every place, and another mission at another time might be more successful.

For the days we were in Cebu, we adapted to the situation, and as usual, adventure found us, bonding us tightly to each other in ways that made up for the distant reception we received. The tropical rain kept us running. Our team rode through the city one afternoon on three small tourist buses, and people crowded onto the open-topped one in front to get the view from the roof. Midway through, the skies opened up and those of us in the back of the caravan watched as our drenched colleagues slid around the flooded bus deck, scrambling to climb inside. Another day's downpour came as we sat on a boat waiting for dinner, and we felt ourselves sinking lower and lower in the water as the deluge continued.

Even the hospital wasn't immune from inundation. Many areas were open-air, and at one point, storm water rushed into the wards, where sixty or more patients lay on cots, with family members at their sides. As the water rose over the tops of our shoes and climbed the wheels of the beds, our internists ran to grab brooms to sweep out the tide—and it wasn't even the rainy season.

The Philippines isn't one of the world's poorest countries, but outside the big city, it had certain similarities to them. Even basic treatment for injuries was makeshift and primitive. Don Longjohn remembers seeing doctors repair a fracture using traction that involved putting a pin through a bone, tying twine to it, and attaching it to a plastic jug filled with sand, or a collection of old pipe fittings.

Power outages were common. One afternoon, Jeri ran down to the lab to pick up blood that we needed in the O.R., and on her way back, her elevator stopped between floors. "We were about to leave for the hotel," she remembers, "and just that morning I had given a strong lecture about how we all needed to be on time for the bus because it can't leave unless the whole team is there. So the elevator stops and I start trying to find an alarm bell or a phone so someone can come get me out, and of course, there's nothing. I'm pounding on the door and it's like a hot box in there. I'm sweating and time is passing, and I'm even thinking, 'What if I have to drink the blood?' I found out later that all the power was off, and in the middle of all that, no one was looking for me."

For me, one of the outages came at an even worse time. I had just started a total knee replacement and gotten as far as making an incision to release the ligaments and expose the inside of the knee. I'd just taken out most of the menisci (the knee cartilage that separates the shin bone and the thigh bone), and that's when the room went dark. I paused, expecting a generator to start up or the power to come back on, but after a few minutes, I realized that that wasn't going to happen. Now I had a dilemma. The work I had already done meant that there was no easy option for this knee—it wouldn't function anymore if I just closed the wound. I asked Julio Raya, our anesthesiologist, if the patient was stable or we needed to stop, and I was relieved when he told me she was fine and I could continue, if I could figure out how. She'd received spinal anesthesia, so there was no concern for her safety.

Mary Ellen ran out of the room and returned with a flashlight. So did Longjohn, whose small, lithium-powered police flashlight was a godsend in the pitch black room. I sat on a stool while I operated so Mary Ellen could hold her light over my shoulder, and when I needed a new tool, she'd swing the beam over to the instrument tray so my assistant Rudy could see what he was giving me. I was relieved to be able to prepare the bone with my usual power tools instead of returning to the manual technique I used in Nepal, and once I finished the bone cuts, I put trial implants on the bone to be sure the knee ligaments were balanced. Fortunately they were—that would save us time. We mixed our bone cement, attached the real implants to the bone, and waited the fifteen minutes till the cement set. Then we released the tourniquet we'd put on the leg, coagulated any spurting bleeders, and sewed up the layers of tissue below the skin with sutures, using staples to close the skin.

These steps took an hour, and the flashlight beam was still strong at the end. We moved the patient from the still dark O.R. into the hallway, which had light coming in from the windows, and then into the recovery room, where the lights were on. We cancelled the rest of the surgery for that day. As far as I knew, I'd done the only total knee replacement ever performed by flashlight, and one seemed like more than enough.

There was one more memorable patient on this trip, a woman who had the same complex hip disease we'd seen in a young woman in Cuba, which essentially prevented her from opening her thighs. At the initial clinic evaluation, the doctors rejected her case saying we didn't have the proper instruments for an operation like hers, but our physical therapist Jennifer Okuno, who was becoming a mainstay of our Op Walk team, was moved when she heard how much the woman longed to be a mother and presented her case to me when I got in from Manila. I agreed to do her double hip replacement, and I've learned from Jennifer, who has stayed in touch with the patient, that the woman now has children and a happy family.

As we make do with the tools at hand on Operation Walk and find ways to do our best work within the limits of the location, many of us realize that despite it all, we're always rich in what will always enable us to adapt—our healer's instinct to love. Our nurse Ashley Trueblood, who joined us in Cebu for her initial mission, expressed it well: "One of the fears and insecurities I had on my first Op Walk trip was if I'd still be a great nurse without all the resources and state-of-the-art equipment. What I learned was that the most important tools in nursing are an open heart and compassion for others, and as long as I have those packed, I can be a world-class caregiver anywhere. We only operated thirteen patients but the patients we did operate will not forget we came."

After Cebu, Jeri and Mary Ellen tweaked their pre-planning checklist and routine even further to help ensure that we'd be welcome and efficient the next time we ventured out. We began getting more assurances and details in writing before we took on a mission—for instance we started asking the hospital administration for a written agreement that it would support Op Walk and help us reach our target number of patients. If a hospital outsider suggested an Op Walk destination, we looked for an enthusiastic backer on the *inside* before committing. We also worked on squeezing some of the chaos out of our process with small additions like asking surgeons to send us the X-rays of prospective patients so we could gauge the size of the implants we would need.

Always learning on every front, we even shifted the way we planned group meals. Though we'd carefully located restaurants beforehand, reviewing menus and negotiating group rates, Cebu taught us that we had neglected to nail down a key service detail—getting food fast. Our tables were bare when we'd shown up at one of our restaurants, and by the time dinner appeared, our hungry troupe had filled up on beer and run up a substantial bar tab, so now we tell restaurants that our party of forty to fifty needs at least salad on the table when we get there. It's a small detail, but it gives us one less headache to deal with. That's our policy: we don't make a mistake or have a misadventure without learning from it and using it to benefit our operations the next time.

## A Personal Meeting with the Mother of Invention

That philosophy got quite a workout in my regular practice when we returned from Cebu City and were thrown back into the ongoing turmoil surrounding the defective Inter-Op cup. All of us in the office had to find a way not just to help our patients but to keep the practice, and ourselves, going.

The pressure was relentless, but looking back, I can see how fertile a period this was for us and how much innovation came out of the problem-solving we had to do. Because I was tended to by a country doctor in my small Iowa hometown, I've always held that model as a professional ideal. I never forgot the way a nurse from Dr. Burns' office came to the house at midnight for two weeks to give me a penicillin shot when I had strep throat in the 1940s, and I had tried to keep that kind of caring in my own practice.

We had always followed up with patients long after surgery, and I made a point of having Jeri make regular phone calls to anyone who had a difficult experience of any kind—a less than optimal result, a complication of some sort. I treated those patients as though they were my own mother, offering the care I'd want her to have. I realized early on that having the experience of feeling cared about helps patients heal and improves their feeling of satisfaction about their procedures. Calls, cards and visits from us worked like medicine, so they were part of our routine.

Now I had more than a hundred distressed patients who'd experienced the shock of either having their hip replacements fail, or being warned that they were likely to, and we put everything we had into making their healing process as easy and positive as possible. After revision surgery, I began sending Jeri out to patients' homes to check on them. In the era before home health care services were readily available, it truly was a throwback to another time. Every Tuesday, she'd make the rounds of patients who'd had surgery the week before, removing sutures, checking blood pressure and looking for blood clots, going over their exercises. Getting into a car the week after surgery to drive to our offices could be tough—why should they have to do that?

I made house calls too, checking the joints, listening to concerns, and offering silent prayers and vocal encouragement. Again and again we said, "We'll see you through this. We'll get you through it." And we did, looking for anything we could do to raise patients' levels of comfort.

Seeing our annual patient load drop from our usual 700 to a fraction of that, we had time on our hands, and when we weren't answering questions from FDA examiners about the recalled cup and tending our affected patients, I wanted us to reach beyond Los Angeles and introduce ourselves more directly to the public. I'd been one of the most visible members of the orthopedic community for decades, but our office had never done a lot of one-to-one outreach beyond that. I asked Jeri to make calls and send out letters and flyers offering arthritis talks, in which she or I or a surgeon or rheumatologist from the practice would offer our expertise on the disease and its treatments to people who might be interested. We contacted retired employees of institutions and companies—the retirees of the Bank of America, say—along with service organizations, civic and seniors' groups, and community centers. Evenings and weekends, we'd be somewhere in the area that stretched north and south from Bakersfield to San Diego and east to Palm Springs, talking about arthritis and joint replacement and answering questions from ten to 200 or more people. We'd also drop in mentions of our experiences with Operation Walk, and linger to get a feel for life outside the confines of metro L.A.

What looked from the outside like a fallow time was a period of rebuilding, meeting good people, and letting them see who we were. Word steadily got out about us and about Op Walk, and we spread our wings in ways we'd never thought to before. New patients began seeking us out, and interest in Operation Walk grew. That's not to say that either the practice or I rebounded seamlessly from the ongoing stresses of the year. Both Jeri and my wife Marilyn let me know I was grouchy, preoccupied and short with them, and when the people you're closest to in your work life *and* your personal life start asking you if you want them there, you know it's time to regroup, and maybe apologize. I did my best to do both.

## Another Crisis, Another Vehicle for Hope

Fall arrived, bringing the terrible shock of the September 11 terrorist attacks. I feared for our country, our loved ones, our charity. Jeri's son was in his second year of Army service, stationed overseas, and all of us were concerned about him, worrying with her, listening for news. The trip we were planning for February, a joint mission with Merrill Ritter's Indiana group that would take us to Nicaragua for the first time, looked dicey. Building goodwill seemed like an important response to the troubles of the world, but we had no idea when we'd be able to travel freely again.

It was in this environment that we decided to bring Operation Walk's healing efforts to those in need at home. We'd been talking about it ever since we returned from China, because conversations about Op Walk often seemed to trigger comments about need in the U.S. As she played in golf tournaments around Los Angeles, Marilyn kept hearing people say, "Operation Walk is great, but why aren't you helping our own poor?" Our colleagues would congratulate us on our humanitarian work and then quickly remind us of the large number of U.S. residents who did not have insurance or adequate health care. In my own practice I frequently saw patients who couldn't have the operations they desperately needed, because without insurance, the out-of-pocket costs were too high. The only option was to refer them to Rancho Los Amigos hospital, part of the county health system, where hip and knee replacement was available at low or no cost to those in need. The care was top-notch and compassionate—Don Longjohn, the lead surgeon there, had gone with us on several Operation Walk trips, including our first mission to Cuba, but there was a two-year wait for the surgery at his hospital because the system was overwhelmed.

Almost daily, there were stories in the newspaper about the number of uninsured people in the U.S. and the callousness of the medical profession to this problem. I considered that criticism unfair because it wasn't doctors who had control over access to care and our reimbursement was declining year by year, which left most practices scrambling to balance expenses and income, but we had to do what we could to address the problem, and I awoke to the fact that for Operation Walk to be respected, we needed to help our own citizens too. It was only right, so, Jeri and Mary Ellen began planning the first Operation Walk in the U.S. We tried to recruit other cities to join us, but doctors feared that patients would sue them for malpractice if there were any complications, so they said they couldn't participate.

Fortunately, we quickly got permission to use Centinela Hospital in Inglewood, a small city just outside of LAX. Centinela was owned by Tenet Healthcare Corp., which knew me from USC, and the hospital's administrator, Mike Rembis, was enthusiastic about our plan. Securing a hospital's cooperation was pivotal because they had to provide the operating rooms, the personnel and patient stay time, and they would assume legal responsibility, as well. Once we secured that, we recruited hospital staff to donate a weekend's worth of vacation time and rounded up donations of medicines, rehab equipment, and implants for the eleven patients Centinela set as a workable target.

We put out a call for patients as we gave our community presentations and sent notices to area rheumatologists inviting them to refer people to the program. Jeri also contacted Telemundo, the Spanish-language TV broadcaster, whose reports on the mission sent 400 people to the phone to call us. We asked each of them to write us letters describing their condition, and Jeri read them all, looking for people with hip or knee arthritis. She sent the best candidates to our doctors to be sure they were medically qualified, but first we had to screen them financially because in the U.S., we were subject to restrictions imposed by the government: it was illegal to operate for free on any patient who had coverage from Medi-Cal, the California version of Medicaid, which helps cover the cost of medical care for people of limited resources.

We'd have to confine our services to those who were poor enough to need our help but not poor enough to be eligible for Medi-Cal—and there were many, a mix of immigrants without Green Cards and citizens without health coverage. There were vast numbers of the working poor and people who made a more-than-subsistence living as hair dressers or gardeners or house cleaners or freelancers but couldn't prioritize insurance and would never have found the $30,000 to $50,000 to cover a hip replacement—it was more than they'd pay for a car.

We winnowed the pool of applicants to the final eleven, feeling privileged to end what had been a traumatic year for everyone on a note of hope.

When Operation Walk "landed" at Centinela on the first weekend in December, one of the patients was Pastor Harold Dewberry, the Australia-born leader of a recovery-focused ministry. Harold, whose osteoarthritis had left him with a severe limp, could walk only short distances when we met him, but our Op Walk team replaced both of his hips, and for the first time in years he could function normally.

"I am so thankful that someone had it in their heart to look at someone like me and help me," he told us. "This is truly a gift from God."

I felt that way too. Bringing Op Walk home let us leave 2001 behind. We were centered in our mission, determined to keep getting up, keep finding new ways to serve patients. For me, the wonder of being a doctor is meeting people in need whose whole bodies seem defeated because of their pain and circumstances, and seeing them emerge after surgery confident, straight, and smiling. Delivering a "miracle" for them never fails to create a miracle in me.

My original notion of Operation Walk took shape after a visit to a Moscow hospital and a meeting with former cosmonaut Valentina Tershkova, the first woman in space. She's beside me inside a training module on a tour of Star City, the cosmonaut training center.

In selecting my first surgical team for the fledgling Op Walk, I turned to lifelong friends from my Des Moines days, Ron Sandler, left, and Bob Porter, right.

Renowned Indiana surgeon Merrill Ritter, right, with our Cuban host Dr. Alfredo Ceballos, fielded some of our most difficult cases. He found a life's mission in humanitarian work on the first Cuba trip.

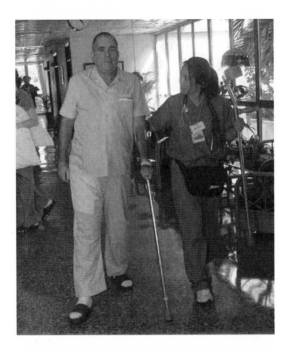

Physical therapist Jennifer Okuno walks the halls with a Cuban patient.

Our first mission to Cuba left me a changed man, feeling a depth of joy I never expected. Kyle Baldwin, our lead physical therapist is at left, with Dr. Alfredo Ceballos at right.

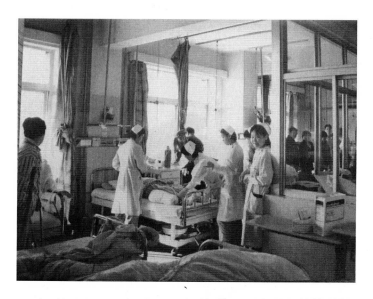

On our second mission, which took us to Friendship Hospital in Beijing, is credited with popularizing the idea of total joint replacement in China.

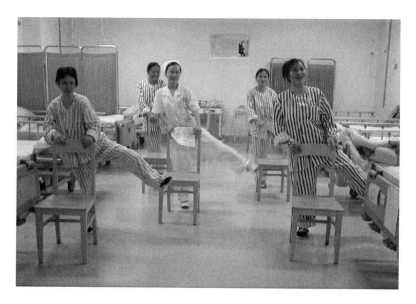

While patients on our first China mission were fearful and suspicious of us and our surgery, trust and familiarity steadily grew. By 2005, our physical therapists had them smiling in the ward before surgery as they practiced the exercises they'd do during recovery.

The poverty we encountered in Kathmandu, Nepal was unlike anything we'd seen.

The Kathmandu hospital had been a carpet factory and was still being converted.

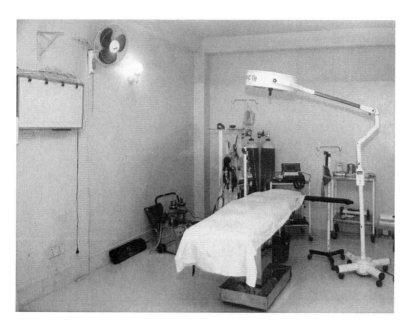

Facilities were minimal in the Nepal operating rooms, and lighting was dim. We carried in our own portable operating lights.

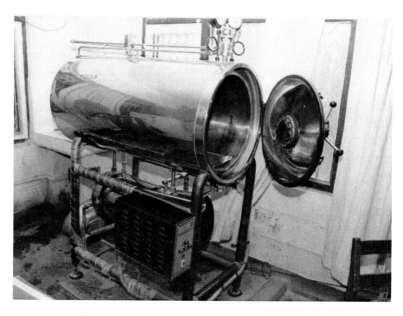

An ancient sterilizer had to suffice.

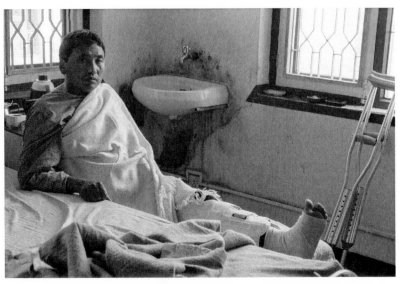

Our first Kathmandu patients were very poor, very brave, very grateful.

Whole families accompanied our potential patients to processing in Kathmandu, which has become a regular Op Walk destination.

Lynne Zawacki and Jeri Ward with staff in Nepal.

In the wards in Cebu City, Philippines, a sunny moment with patients between downpours.

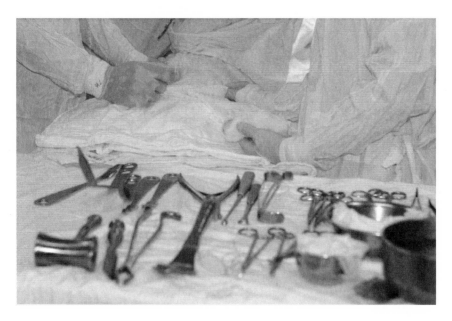

Instruments ready for surgery.

Each trip literally took tons of equipment and supplies. If we were lucky, it would be waiting at the hospital for us. If not, there would be wrangling for us to do.

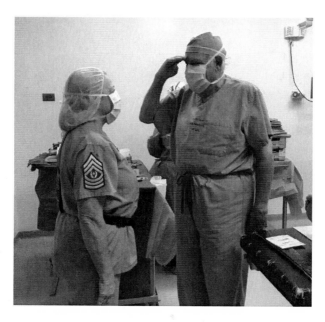

Everyone knew who kept things spinning like a top in the O.R. Mary Ellen Sieben made sure we were organized, efficient and had whatever we needed to handle anything that came up.

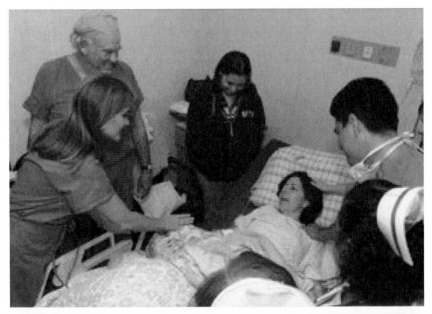

The goodwill our work created made us ambassadors for the U.S., and occasionally, dignitaries came calling. First Lady Vivian Torrijos of Panama met us and visited every Op Walk patient on the Panama City wards. In 2015, Fidel Castro thanked our team for three hours in Spanish.

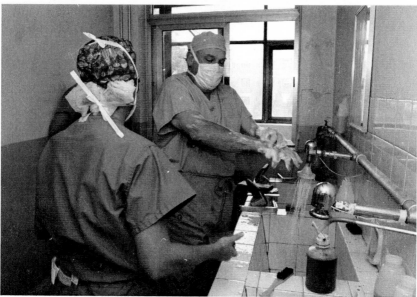

Facilities were simple in Managua. Physical therapist Vivienne Uytana used the area behind the hospital for stair training with patient Maria Josefa Meja. I did my washing up in a very basic scrub sink.

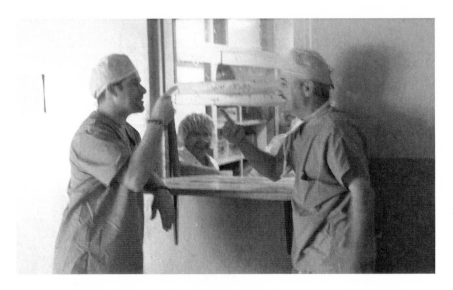

Manning central sterile in Managua are biomed technician Matt Sandusky and central sterile chief Ferli Zoumalie.

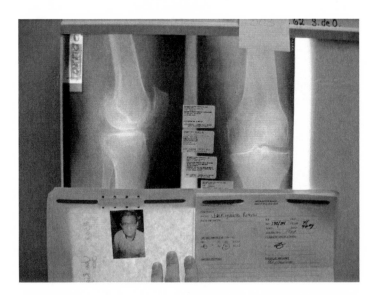

On our first mission to Cuba we identified patients with name bands on their arms. We began adding patient photos to our files of medical histories and X-rays when we realized how many people had similar names. There are many Marias and Josés, and so many Sanchezes and Garcias in a place like Nicaragua or El Salvador.

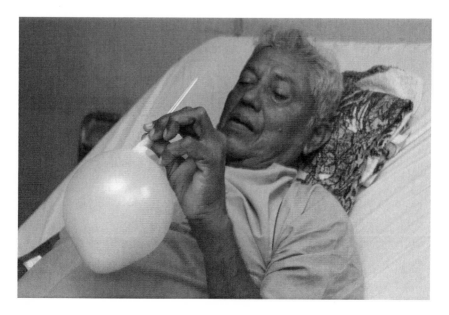

With no access to complicated equipment, patients learn to do breathing exercises by blowing through straws attached to balloons.

We met often between surgeries to check and update the schedule, making notes and changes and checking in.

The Hermano Pedro Hospital in Antigua is a converted church that serves as a base for dozens of relief missions. It's become one of our favorite destinations.

Our team and patients gather during a 2006 mission in Antigua. In the front row: Dr. Jonathan (Jondy) Cohen and his wife Rocki, who provided major support for the trip in honor of Jondy's mother Jean Hide-Cohen.

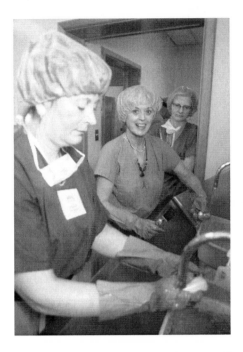

Our "dishwashing" crew cleans instruments in Antigua. From front, Jennifer Desanto, Marilyn Dorr, and Rita Sandler.

Jeri and me, pausing to breathe.

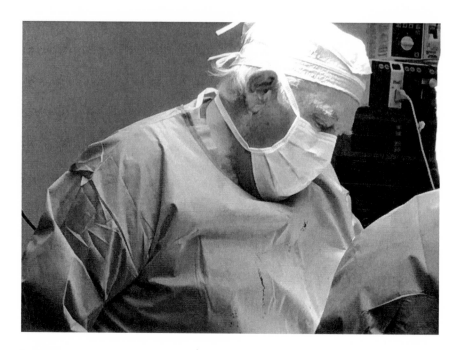

In surgery.

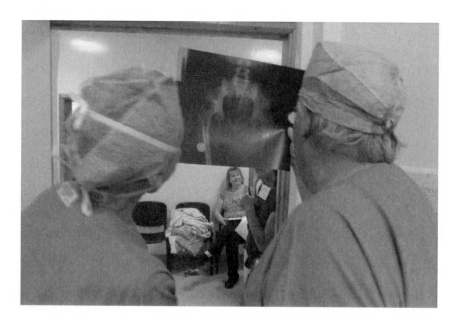

Consulting between operations, Jeri in the background.

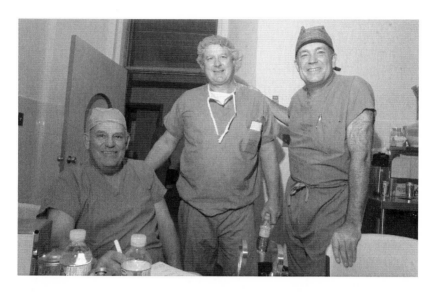

In Antigua, Guatemala with Dr. Aaron Hofmann, center, and Dr. Brian Parsley.

Around the dinner table in Antigua, left to right, Dr. Aaron Hofmann, me, Padre Jose, and our anesthesiologist Julio Raya. Standing, left to right, Yuji Hishiki, scrub tech; Lisa Fujimoto, my physician assistant; Rosanna Springer, circulating nurse, Rudy Costales, our surgical scrub tech, Frankie Luczon, scrub tech; Ferli Zoumalie, CST.

The back door of the Sonsonate hospital opened onto a vibrant street market.

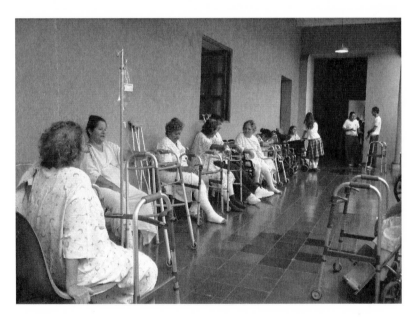

Sonsonate patients gather in the courtyard for rest and mutual encouragement.

Families wait in a Sonsonate hallway as a patient tests his new joints.

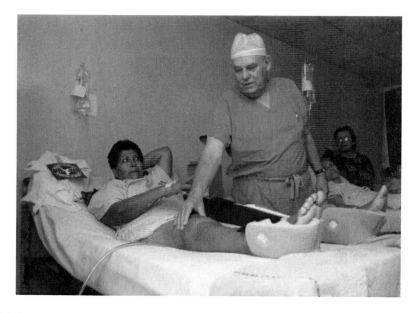

Making rounds, checking on the status of a patient's unoperated knee.

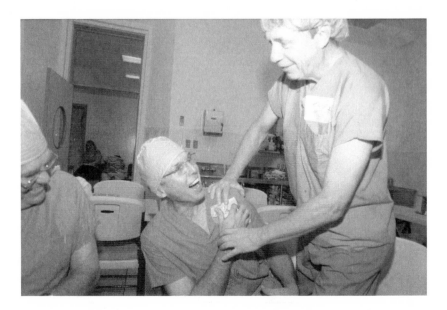

Canadian surgeons and good friends Dr. Bob Bourne and Dr. Cecil Rorabeck founded our first international Op Walk chapter and often take teams to Guatemala.

Operation Walk broke new ground with WOGO, a team led by women surgeons. Pictured are founding members Dr. Robyn Hakanson, Dr. Audrey Tsao, Dr. Amanda Marshall Rodriguez, and Dr. Rinelda Horton.

Jeri and Mary Ellen take pre-mission trips to size up locales. They filled notebooks with details on a preliminary trip to Saigon.

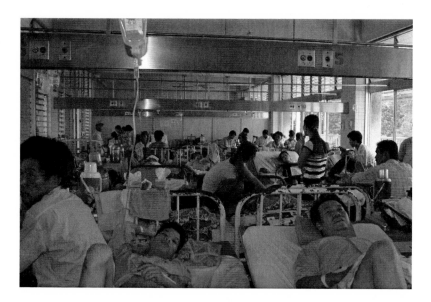

In the crowded Saigon wards, we made sure all our patients' beds had wheels so we could roll patients out to the hallways and put them on gurneys to take them to surgery.

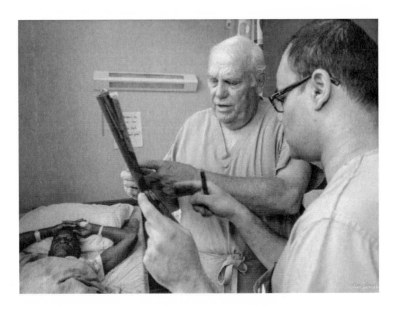

Our first Op Walk mission to Africa took us to Tanzania, where many patients were Maasai. I consulted on a case with one of my former fellows, Dr. Aamer Malik.

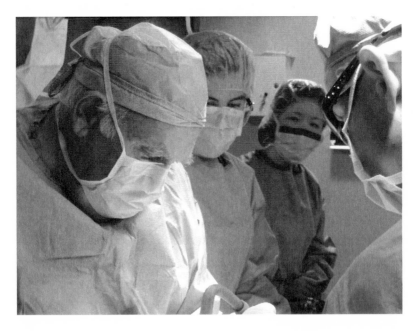

In the O.R. in Tanzania.

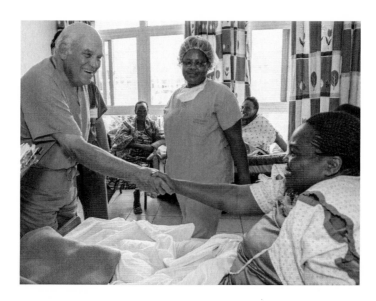

Post-surgery rounds.

Our Tanzanian patients were exceptionally warm. This is what joy and healing look like.

We planted a tiny sapling in Cuba on our first Operation Walk mission. Four decades later, when I returned to see it with Alfredo Ceballos, Jeri and Mary Ellen, I was stunned to see how it had flourished—just like Op Walk.

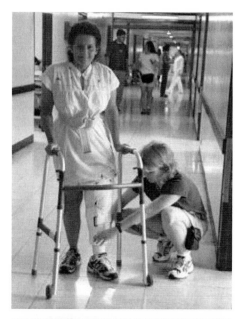

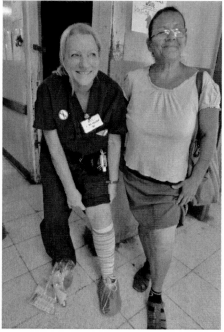

Escarleth Meza, top, with PT Lynn Loxterman. I replaced Escarleth's knee after a crippling injury and years later, she came by to cheer Mary Ellen, who'd had her own knee replaced.

For Rogelio Montepeque Estrada, having worn-out knees meant losing his ability to work. He tried for years to get help, and I was privileged to be able to do his surgery.

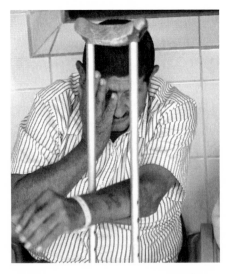

Exhaustion and worry overtake Rogelio as he waits.

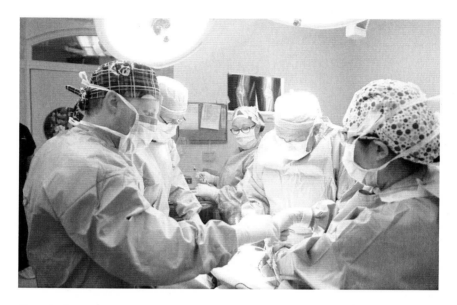

Rogelio's surgery.

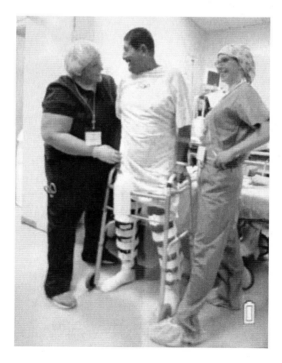

Rogelio stands tall on his new legs.

The joy of my work is immeasurable. I am a happy man.

Finishing one mission, Jeri and I are on to the next. Every ending is a new beginning.

**All photos courtesy of the Operation Walk participants who were with us on our journey. Special thanks to photographers Jim Morris and Mike Smith, who helped us document the early years, and to Cami Ward and Pablo Ortega, who have recorded the later ones.**

# CHAPTER 6:

## Years of Innovation, Nicaragua and Beyond

································································

We were as surprised as anyone when our Nicaragua trip came off as planned despite the disruptions to travel and security fears that were still rippling through the system in the wake of September 11. Despite some nerves, we were excited to go. The mission to Managua had been a long time coming. We had first come in contact with Nicaraguan surgeons in Havana, where they were working among the Cuban medical staff, but we'd hesitated to accept earlier invitations to take Operation Walk there. Finally, though, we'd found strong enough contacts in Managua to believe that we could succeed.

That's not to say it wouldn't be challenging. Nicaragua was still struggling back to its feet after a long and expensive civil war, and Hospital Escuela Dr. Roberto Calderon Gutierrez, the hospital for the indigent where we would be working, was as poor as the patients we'd be serving. Our pre-trip reconnaissance let us know that we'd have to scramble to create the baseline conditions we needed for patient safety. For a start, the all-important autoclaves—those finicky and essential "ovens" we use to sterilize our metal tools and devices—were out of commission. In Havana, we had been able to simply change the settings on working machines to bring them to our standards, but the large old Russian models that served this hospital weren't even plugged in. Nurses disinfected medical tools by piling them into a metal pan and haphazardly soaking them in a disinfectant that we thought might be iodine, so we hunted down parts for the rundown machines and coaxed them back into working order before our teams arrived.

There was other basic prep to do as well. Jeri noticed that some of the beds in the wards were missing mattresses and arranged for our home hospital, which was going through a regular mattress update, to send thirty or so of the old ones to Managua. Wheelchairs and gurneys needed wheels, so we packed extra parts for repairs. We even brought in chains so we could anchor the large oxygen tanks Mary Ellen had noticed standing unsecured against the walls. They were an extreme fire hazard in an area where volcanoes and earthquakes are always rumbling.

A welcome find on that first scouting trip was Mauricio Manzanarez who drove and translated for Jeri and Mary Ellen. Mauricio is the busy operations manager for Threefold Ministries, a Canadian charity, but he was happy to assist us and has become a valued part of Op Walk missions to Managua. Translators are our ears on the ground wherever we go, and Jeri always asks that they listen during meetings and truthfully let us know anything that was said but not directly conveyed to us. When people are eager for our help, it's common for them to tell us what they think we want to hear, rather than being candid, which can complicate our planning. When we ask hospital administrators if they have, say, a nitrogen tank to run our high-speed drill, they may know they don't but give us a vague answer because they think that if they say no, we'll decide not to come. A translator like Mauricio can fill in the gaps for us so we can circle back later and do the problem-solving that will help us get what we need.

Where we can, we like to get an idea of how our patients are living so we can help provide what they'll need for the best recovery. After showing Jeri and Mary Ellen the crater of the nearby Masaya volcano, our host, Dr. Rene´ Quesada, took them to the shores of Lake Managua. Lean-to dwellings of cardboard and tin connected by muddy roads sprawled along the water. Sewage pipes had emptied into the lake for years, and the area smelled like it. They pulled up to a house to chat with a couple who had a baby and three school-aged children, and as Jeri and Mary Ellen stood talking with them, the kids ran inside, emerging a couple of minutes later dressed in their Catholic school uniforms, excited to show off that they were going to school. We could see from the photos that Jeri brought home that they were filthy, but they were full of pride.

Part of what we understand, and emphasize to our teams, is that along with everything else we see, we need to see and respect the pride. As Jeri always reminds us, some of the very poorest people we meet don't look at themselves as being poor—they're just living the lives they have. We all want to feel good, to eat, to have a roof over our heads and some of the roofs that make people feel happy aren't anything like what we're used to. My own circumstances are much more fortunate than those I've seen on Op Walk, but as someone who grew up not realizing that my family was considered to be poor and might've felt diminished by the label, I know the truth of what she's saying.

There was no shortage of patients on this mission. The screening clinic was packed. Some people had traveled two days by bus from villages in the mountains and some came haltingly on foot. One elderly man could not walk to the clinic because of his arthritis, so his son carried him on his back, the father's arms around the son's neck, and the son hunched forward so the father's legs wouldn't drag on the ground. I watched them move slowly from the waiting area to an examining room, more certain than ever of why we'd come.

A few miles away, Merrill Ritter's Indiana team was assessing patients at Hospital Escuela Militar Dr. Alejandro Dávila Bolaños. The official who'd persuaded us to come to Nicaragua wanted all of us to work out of the more modern military hospital, but I was concerned that the patients there might be more well off than the ones we usually focus on and that we were being asked to overlook the needy. Ultimately, though, we couldn't deny that the patients at Bolaños had to be suffering too. Merrill Ritter and his group, who had planned to work alongside us on this trip, decided they'd go to Bolaños and handle a full caseload on their own. For their first largely independent trip, I was glad to have them in slightly less dire conditions than we veterans would be juggling. We'd all still be in the same hotel, sharing some meals, and I would be teaching with Ritter at a symposium for the local doctors. The Indiana team knew they could call on us for back-up, but they'd be running their own show.

So soon after the September 11 attacks, we felt unusually conspicuous, and we were especially conscious of not wanting to be raucous or even loud as we sat in a lobby, bar or restaurant. We didn't want to be ugly Americans, and we didn't want to make ourselves targets. We decided it made sense to stay in after dark, and after our first night in a Ramada Inn-like hotel left us feeling cooped up with little to do, Jeri struck a deal with the Intercontinental Hotel, which was closer to the hospital and more pleasant for the volunteers, who were giving up their vacation time to help us. Jeri, who drives a persuasive bargain, made sure the upgrade would come at a reasonable price. As it turned out, the winning amenity turned out to be quite basic: television. Both Indiana and L.A. were headed for the NBA playoffs that year, so we used that as an occasion to unwind—and stay safe—as we gathered in our rooms to cheer them on.

## A Challenge to Savor: Escarleth's Knee

The level of pain and deformity I saw in our patients was sometimes extreme. It was on this trip that I performed some of the most difficult surgeries I'd ever encounter on Operation Walk. Earlier, I mentioned Escarleth, a woman whose knee had been dislocated when soccer-playing kids knocked down a wall of her house and it fell on top of her. She had suffered for two years with her debilitating, untreated injury, and when she came into the clinic, the surgeon conducting the preliminary screening recommended that we not take her case. It wasn't that she had underlying conditions that would put her at risk during surgery. The problem was that the operation itself appeared to be so difficult that the surgeon felt he couldn't do it safely. To be honest, there weren't many of us who would take it on.

Escarleth's anatomy had been badly distorted. The knee joins the bottom end of the femur (thigh bone) and the top of the tibia (shin bone), and when it is dislocated and the femur is pushed forward over the front of the tibia, the ligaments holding the joint together all tear. The main artery and nerve for the leg, which run from hip to ankle behind the knee, are displaced too.

Escarleth was lucky that her artery hadn't been torn in the accident, because she would have required emergency surgery and risked losing her lower leg if circulation weren't restored. Performing the kind of surgery she needed would put the artery at risk again. Her body had produced scar tissue to fill the new gap between the femur and the tibia, and her leg artery and nerve were now buried somewhere inside it. To repair Escarleth's knee, we'd have to remove that scar tissue without damaging the embedded nerve and artery. If we cut either one, we might have to amputate her leg. The prospects were daunting, but I had operated on thousands of knees and performed a knee replacement on a dislocated knee once before. Early in my long career, I'd worked on plenty of patients who had suffered with arthritis for many years and had severely damaged joints. So taking my prerogative as the senior surgeon on the mission, I okayed the case, and signed on to do it myself.

Escarleth's operation was so complex and unusual that the local medical students, residents, and attending surgeons all wanted to observe. We set up cameras in the O.R. so they could watch from a remote conference room, which would give them a better view of the operating field than they'd probably have if they were in the room. My nerves jangled as I began because although I was confident, I knew how easily I could fail.

I made my first incision and exposed Escarleth's knee. The highest risk would come right after that, as I opened the skin and fat and encountered the scar tissue. My first concern was to keep from cutting the quadriceps tendon and the patella ligament, which do the work of straightening the leg. I took care to protect them as I removed the scar tissue bit by bit, on constant alert for the nerve and artery. I used a pencil-sized tool called a bovie to precisely direct electrical current at the tissue and cut it by burning and vaporizing it away. If the heated bovie got near a nerve, the nerve would stimulate nearby muscles, which would contract. That would be my warning that I was getting too close. But there would be no similar warning as I approached the crucial artery—I might not know it was there until I nicked it or severed it completely.

Once I finished the front side of the knee I hoped to be able to perch the femur in its normal position on top of the tibia and proceed with the operation, but there was scar tissue *behind* the knee too, and I had to cut that away before I could move the bones into place. Now I had to work even more slowly, taking extreme care as I excised the scar tissue where I now knew the nerve and artery had to be. I picked my way through the minefield, and finally, I was able to align the femur and tibia. The leg was safe.

Breathing easier now, I prepared the bones for their implants and put in a new metal and plastic knee whose design would replace Escarleth's torn ligaments and restore the joint's stability. That was a routine procedure, and it went quickly. When I was done, I bowed out of the operating team and allowed others to close the wound. As I walked into the conference room, the waiting doctors and students chapped and cheered, which is the only time in my entire career that has happened for a high-stakes operation like this. Doctors are not treated like entertainers, and their achievements are generally private. That's as it should be, but I admit I enjoyed the moment of recognition from my peers. Part of the humanity of Operation Walk is that we assist and acknowledge each other in ways we don't often do at home. The success of one is the success of all, and it feels good.

The real reward, though, came the next morning, when Escarleth got up to put our work to the test. Local staff and Op Walk team members gathered in the hallway to see, and I stood directly outside the door to her ward. Her bed was one of six in the room—there were three on each side—and before she could really try out her knee, she'd have to navigate the small space between the beds and get into the middle of the center aisle. Jennifer Okuno, our lead therapist on this trip, guided her into a walker and took a comforting place by her side.

We held our breaths as Escarleth lifted her bandaged leg and let it swing forward. She did not know if this knee would work, and neither did we, but then we saw her moving down the hallway, leaning on her walker with tears running down her cheeks. She was shifting her weight and feeling her new knee flex then stiffen to hold her, and she could walk again after so many difficult months. Jennifer was a veteran of thousands of knee patients, but she couldn't hold back her tears. As Escarleth went slowly past, the crowd in the hallway started clapping, and through the mist clouding my vision I saw her laugh and cry at the same time. I know I was doing that too.

In this moment of pure elation, all of us were excited for the good fortune of someone else. It was the Golden Rule in action.

## Why Not Send People Home to Heal?

In Nicaragua, as in Cuba and Nepal, we continued to be impressed by the way family members attentively looked after their parents and spouses before and after surgery, bringing in food, helping with bathing and dressing, and soaking up every bit of training we could offer about caring for their loved ones at home. We saw the quality of their attention and felt good about entrusting our patients' post-op care to the people closest to them. The strong culture of caring had grown from necessity in the poorest places we'd taken Op Walk, but it was something I thought we could cultivate in our model of patient care at home. I began to think seriously about making home care, by family members when it was feasible, a pillar of a project I'd been contemplating for some time: getting patients out of the hospital more quickly after surgery. That would be a major focus when we got home.

What pushed that effort into high gear for me was seeing Rich Berger, a Chicago-based orthopedist, operate a patient at my Masters Series course and send him home that day. I knew we could do that too. Berger and I were both developing ways to do hip replacements with micro incisions, which made for easier wound care and recovery. The time seemed right for micro hospital stays as well. There would be physical benefits—accidents and infections are both known to be higher in nursing homes and rehab facilities than at home—but some of the greatest rewards would come from the patients' own peace of mind. One of the biggest fears people have when they go into a hospital is that they will lose control of their lives, so it would be a terrific boon for them to be able to return to their familiar environment soon after surgery. Though cost didn't figure at all in our thinking, there could be significant economic savings for the health system too.

I sent Mary Ellen and Jeri to Chicago to shadow Berger's staff and see how his team orchestrated its pre-op planning and post-op care to make that possible, but when they returned, they told me that Rich was still at the stage of sending patients from surgery to a hotel across the street to recover. We didn't have an option like that, and we didn't want to wait for Berger to work out the next part of the plan, so we decided to reverse-engineer a process of our own that would culminate in sending a patient safely home within a day. Jeri and Mary Ellen plunged in with their usual "challenge accepted!" attitude and set about seeing how many levers they'd have to adjust in our usual operation to make same-day release work for everyone. It turned out there were many.

In selecting patients, we knew we'd be looking for those receiving single joint replacements, people who would have supportive family members at home. We'd choose younger patients in good health over those with conditions that might need closer monitoring after surgery. Family support wasn't yet something we assumed would be readily available, but we knew that if we carefully explained the benefits, we could draw family members in and make them part of the recovery plan. It didn't seem unreasonable to ask. In the U.S. we'd limited families to dropping by during visiting hours, and even told them that basic functions like helping their loved ones bathe or dress or exercise required professional staff, but such care has been provided by families in other countries forever, and Operation Walk had opened our eyes to how well that could work. It was a simple idea we could bring home to improve medicine, a lesson from the people we'd gone to teach.

Jeri began asking family members to come along with patients to her pre-op class so they could better understand what the surgery and recovery would look like. They'd also watch and learn from our physical therapists about how to help guide exercises at home. We'd make families the best advocates and support system for their loved ones by making sure they heard everything the doctors, nurses, and therapists told the patient.

The same kind of planning that had served us so well in Operation Walk came into play as Jeri and Mary Ellen worked this new logistical puzzle. For instance, if a patient was set to go home the day of surgery, we'd need to operate them first thing in the morning and use an anesthetic that would wear off enough to let them get up by noon. We'd slot older people who'd be staying in the hospital as the last cases of the day, knowing we wouldn't have to get them up and moving. There were long chains of interconnected details to work out, because this new system came without a manual.

We thought ahead to the equipment that a person would need at home immediately after surgery—a crutch, a raised toilet seat, a walker—and worked to be sure all of it would be available when a patient got there. We couldn't wait until they were on their way home to find out if their insurance would cover the equipment they needed or if the pharmacies near them closed early, keeping them from getting their pain medication until the next day. Handling all that minutiae became part of the pre-op class two weeks ahead of the operation. We identified who would need what equipment and what medicines they'd typically be taking, and got everything pre-ordered and organized so it would be ready for them.

Some of the biggest barriers to changing the long-entrenched system of sending patients for three-to five-day rehab stays were psychological, but we learned to reach past doubts and change people's thinking. When I had a patient who was waffling about going home early I'd say: "Your germs in your home know you and they wonder where you have gone. They are missing you. The germs in my hospital don't know you and they don't want you in their space. They'll likely attack you!" People would chuckle, but they would agree to go home. When family members argued that their mother or father should go to a rehab facility rather than home, I would ask, "Who took care of you when you were little and had measles or mumps?" and provide the answer by looking over at the parent who was now the patient. Reluctant relatives almost always responded by saying, "We'll take care of it."

Staff resistance to our new protocol wasn't something we had anticipated, but when we ran into it, we realized we'd need to get every person who came in contact with our patients on board. In the pre-op class, Jeri would tell patients, "You're going home the same day, and soon after surgery, you're going to get up and walk to the nurse's station and all the way to the end of the hall." I would cheer them on when I spoke with them as well. We found that simply announcing the plan set expectations for what's possible and how things would work. And that was true whether we told them they'd be home and walking the day of their surgery or that they'd be miserable afterwards. As Jeri put it, "If you say, 'You're going to feel bad. Your legs are going to swell up and you're not going to want to get up for three days,' that's what will happen."

That's why it was a problem when a patient in the recovery room told the nurse, "I'm going home today!" only to hear, "Oh no you're not. You just had a hip replacement and you'll be here several days." After that happened a few times, undermining our efforts to give patients confidence in their ability to recover, Jeri began educating the floor nurses and staff members, working with them to explain how to talk to our patients and detailing what we had taught in the pre-op class. We had meetings every two weeks for months until our message was consistent from top to bottom and we had our system working smoothly. I led the charge and motivated everyone while Jeri and Mary Ellen kept refining the operational details that would keep us on track. When we began, we were sending forty percent of our patients to rehab. Within a year, the number was one percent. The other ninety-nine percent were going straight home—and doing well. Jeri kept up her weekly practice of visiting people to check their wounds and exercise routines, which also increased their comfort level.

As word got out about our success, people across the country began calling us just as we'd originally called Berger saying, "Can we come out to watch? Can we sit through your class? Can we see how you train families and patients?" Still, it took time to change the expectations of the medical community at large. For ten years, I was the only person in L.A. sending total hip replacement patients home the same day. I think that reflects what Malcolm Gladwell says about change in *The Tipping Point*: first come the innovators, people like Berger and our practice, then come the early adopters, and then there is a long pause while others wait to see how the new idea will work out.

## Short Stays Come to Operation Walk

It's in my blood to keep innovating, so as soon as we'd succeeded with same-day discharge at home, I took it on the road with Operation Walk. In screening patients, if we saw a healthy forty-five-year-old man who needed a single joint replacement and had a spouse or family at home, we knew we didn't need to keep him in the hospital and worked to release him early. Situations varied widely country to country, of course, and we always worried about infections and wound care, but we made sure our teaching about both was strong, and families proved to be conscientious learners. Very quickly, a twenty-four hour stay got to be the norm for patients under sixty-five who didn't have a lot of health problems. You can see the effect in our mission scrapbooks. We have always taken a group photo of our patients and volunteer teams at the end of each trip, and if you line those portraits up by date, you'll notice that our patient groups shrink over time—not because we were serving fewer people but because in missions after 2003 or '04, most everyone had gone home by the last day. Sometimes patients are in the photo only because they've come back to say goodbye and smile at our cameras.

Local doctors were startled to see us discharging patients so quickly because they were used to long hospitalizations, but they didn't interfere. I suspect they were willing to go along with our new protocols because Operation Walk was a no-fault zone for them. If something went wrong, we, not they, would be to blame, but I don't recall any complications because of early discharge abroad. Family care was good, and so was follow-up from local physicians. Doctors and hospitals at home were slower to adapt. I think part of that was inertia and part had to do with poorer and less confident surgeons worrying about giving patients more control over their recovery. As late as 2014, the average post-op stay in the hospital where I was based was four and a half days. It took two years of seeing our success and then peer pressure from nurses for the surgeons there to change—and they still don't do same-day discharge. Unlike the doctors in Operation Walk countries, who are so hungry to learn and improve, surgeons can get complacent in the U.S., but that often changes when they participate in Op Walk and all of us have a chance to learn from each other. The results we get break through old expectations, and teams often carry new approaches to patient care home with them.

## A Standoff with 'Pirates'

The first Managua trip inspired one of the surgeons who participated, Doug Dennis, to found his own Op Walk team back home in Denver. Now we were three! Doug is a powerhouse in orthopedics, known internationally for his research on knees. He'd come with us bringing a small team from his own hospital, to test the waters and see the L.A. and the Indiana groups in action. Like me, he has strong religious roots, and he'll often say that his favorite Bible verse is Luke 12:48, the essence of which is, "To whom a lot has been given, a lot is expected." A prominent inventor and innovator, he was driven to share the fruits of his success.

Doug and his new Denver team planned to launch in October of 2002, just seven months after Managua, joining us for a training mission to La Paz, Mexico, where Bob Porter, one of our original surgeons, had arranged for us to come. Bob had a home in a town called Los Barriles and knew the surgeons in nearby La Paz well. Mexico, especially the Baja California area, seemed like a natural destination for our L.A. crew. Our city and hospital are filled with people with strong ties to the country, and Baja is so close we were eager to venture down. Excitement was high on the Mexican side as well. The La Paz surgeons were keen to work with us, and we arrived there to find a clinic crowded with patients. I particularly remember the face of an elderly man whose knee deformities had given him severely bowed legs. I kiddingly asked if he had ridden a horse all his life and we became *"compadres."* I promised him I would fix his knees, but to this day his face haunts me because I could not keep my word.

What stood in the way was a cargo problem. We'd seen a lot of those, so while we were concerned when our supplies hadn't arrived by the time our teams did, we thought we could work around the delay. We went to the government agency whose permission and assurances we'd gotten before we left, and when that didn't get results, we decided to go ahead and screen the patients, believing that we could reach high enough into the hierarchy to get our cargo freed. Long into the night, Jeri and I were on the phone with agencies and officials trying to get through to anyone who could help. But after the clinic was finished we received a call telling us that the truck hauling our goods was still on the San Diego side of the border because the Mexican border agents wanted $700,000 to allow entry. They had declared that our humanitarian cargo was worth more than a million dollars, and they were imposing their own astronomical tariff. It was the first time a country had asked us for any duty at all.

I called my cousin Tom Dorr in Washington, D.C., where he was the undersecretary of agriculture for President George Bush, and explained our dilemma. Tom contacted the Mexican ambassador to the U.S., who called to tell me he had connected with the Mexican minister of health. She, in turn, promised to order the border agents to allow the cargo into Mexico. I was confident that we would be delayed a couple more days at most but would accomplish our mission, especially after I received a fax from her with a copy of the instructions she had sent to the border.

However, the border officials never relented and our cargo truck headed back to Los Angeles. I learned then that the provinces in Mexico do not respect the central government, and that local corruption is hard to fight. I told the team to stay and have a holiday, and we paid for their hotel and meals as if they were working. I flew home bitterly disappointed and concerned that the situation might recur in other countries. Fortunately, this was the only time we would encounter mission-ending obstruction of our team or cargo. Unwilling to risk another "hijacking," we've never planned another trip to Mexico.

Seeing the mission cut short was a blow for Doug Dennis's team, but they weren't dissuaded. The next year, they joined us for a trip Managua to give the gift of mobility to thirty-three people, for whom we replaced forty-six total joints. That trip was followed by Denver's first solo mission, in 2004, and they quickly became Operation Walk leaders, taking an average of two trips a year. In an odd twist, the only other time I had to call in my cousin Tom in Washington was to help them with another cargo problem. Doug and his team had gone to Peru, and at the end of their mission, they'd packed their cargo and sent it to customs for clearance to be shipped home. Two months later, when it still hadn't arrived, Doug asked if I could help. I explained the problem to Tom, who went to Karl Rove, President Bush's senior advisor. Rove made a call to Peruvian officials, and within the week the cargo was back in Denver. Once again, we saw the power of our angels, the friends, family, government officials and highly placed people who could smooth the way for us and intervene when problems arise. Thanks to their string-pulling and behind-the-scenes help, glitches don't become crises.

## Big Ideas: Small Incisions, Computer Mapping

In those early years of the 2000s, I never stopped moving. I had gotten curious about using mini-incisions to access the hip joint in 2002 after I saw Tom Sculco of the Hospital for Special Surgery in New York make a presentation at the Hip Society. Instead of the then-customary eighteen or twenty-inch incisions, his were a quarter of that length, yet it didn't take any longer to place the implants through the smaller opening and there was less blood loss, less area open to potential infection, less pain, and quicker recovery. Because it took less time to stop bleeders and close the wound, the operation could be thirty minutes shorter. I was fascinated, and afterward, I had dinner with Tom, a good friend. He told me I had to try it myself—so I did.

Over the course of a month, I gradually shortened my incision, and I changed the position of it compared to Tom's. I wrote about my technique early and demonstrated it with live surgery so that I became Tom's wing man for it, gaining international respect in the process. I designed instruments to make the operation tissue-friendly and then wrote the definitive textbook on the technique. It's been the most studied and successful minimally invasive surgery for total hip replacement, but it's not the only one. Over in Chicago, Rich Berger was pioneering the use of a small incision through the front of the hip and finding success with that. Both of us were constantly looking for ways to advance our surgery and improve our patients' outcomes, so it was no surprise that he made that leap from micro incisions to "micro" hospital stays and prompted us to attempt it. The Masters lecture series was an incubator and cross-pollinator that let innovators keep learning from each other and Op Walk let us carry many of those innovations into the world.

I kept my foot on the accelerator in those years with research into using computer-assisted navigation in hip replacements. I was an early advocate of computer navigation, and in 2003 I began testing the real-world performance of a system designed to guide surgeons in the tricky placement of the implant cup that fits into the acetabulum, that hard-to-see socket of the hip joint. Using light-emitting diodes to mark reference points on and outside the body, reflectors that could track the movement of surgical instruments, and an antenna pointer that could mark the position of the implant, we could transmit positioning information to a computer, which created maps for surgeons to steer by. Touching the pointer to the edges of a holder for the implant's cup, we could see and refine its position before the cup went in. If the system worked, it would give us a view into the body that we'd never had before, and help us improve the angle of the implant for better fit and wear. Researchers had already shown that doing CT scans before surgery and using the positioning information gained from the images significantly improved surgeons' ability to place the cup accurately, but doing CT scans before every operation seemed impractical in most busy practices. We hoped the computer system we were testing would be easier to use.

My study aimed to answer many questions, including the most basic ones: was the computer's guidance more accurate than an experienced surgeon's intuition? How would the system perform in real life? How could it be better? I got the permission of 159 patients to find out. I personally operated all of them between February 2003 and October 2004, implanting cups as usual and measuring my own accuracy in eighty-five of the hips. In the remaining patients, I adjusted the placement of the cup with the help of the computer. In the process, we learned the kinds of things you can only find out in practice: those reference-point diodes stuck to the body can shift and fall off in the pounding of surgery, and it helps to mark key spots with dye so you can find them again, as well as grounding one of the most important positional markers by pounding it into bone. We found that it was vital to measure the tilt of the pelvis precisely for the system to work, and we figured out how to do that. We also learned that when the measurements were precise and markers were correctly placed, computer positioning was more accurate than what I could achieve with my practiced eye. We published our results in 2005 and I've been a strong advocate of computer navigation as it has evolved in the years since then.

## The View from Under the Knife

In the midst of all this, I experienced total hip replacement from the other side of the scalpel. My mentor, Chit Ranawat, was in L.A. for a conference of 1,500 surgeons, where he demonstrated a total knee replacement and I showed my micro-incision technique in a demonstration broadcast from my hospital. Afterward, Chit stayed the night with Marilyn and me, and the next morning, he did my hip surgery. It was widely talked about in orthopedics circles because the salesmen for the company that sold Chit's hip system were bragging to surgeons that I was going to get *his* implant instead of my own. Chit had other plans, and though he generally used devices he'd designed when he did surgery, for this procedure, he used mine. He warmed up by using it five times in New York before he arrived—to get to know it better— and then operated with my surgical partner, William Long, who used my design all the time, to put it into me. That shut up the industry—and we had fun joking about it. My surgery and its outcome were flawless, something that didn't go unnoticed in the orthopedics community.

What was it like being on the receiving end of the surgery that was so familiar to me? Interestingly, I didn't learn much that I could apply to Operation Walk, but my Op Walk experience influenced the way I planned my recovery. I used pre-emptive medication to prevent pain, as we do on our missions (I didn't use pain medicine after the second day post-op), and I followed the same-day release protocol that we'd worked so hard to master. I was up and walking, then out of the hospital, the afternoon of my surgery. Jeri and I have long prided ourselves on getting back to work as quickly as possible after the various medical treatments we've had over the years, and I walked, healed, and was back in action almost before anyone realized I was gone. My patients loved the fact that I had had my own hip replaced. Somehow, even though I'd invented their implants and developed the surgical techniques I was using on them, knowing first-hand what they were experiencing gave me a new kind of authority when we talked about their recovery.

## Angels in Very High Places

Op Walk's reputation continued to grow abroad. In 2004, Fidel Castro's son, an orthopedic surgeon, operated with our team in Havana, giving us the ultimate angel in Cuba—Fidel himself. Perhaps even more influential, in its way, was an operation I did during that trip on the 60-year-old manager of an immensely popular band called Los Van Van. After small-incision surgery, we sent the manager home the same day, and that night, he was the talk of a party I attended at the home of Pablo Milanés, a huge singing star in the Caribbean. (Milanés later sought me out in Los Angeles to replace his own hip.)

I was always happy to operate a few patients on Op Walk like the Van Van manager because they could afford to donate the cost of their operation to the hospital or to Op Walk, which would cover a significant chunk of a mission's expenses. And if they talked about their experience and helped give people a greater sense of confidence in total joint replacement or the idea of a short hospital stay, all the better.

Research fed innovation, which fed Op Walk, and Op Walk never ceased to feed and sustain our energy and our spirits. We were our own perpetual motion machine.

# CHAPTER 7:

## Growth Years:
## Now They Know Who We Are

........................................................................

Sometimes at odd moments, I see myself back in the small towns of Iowa where I grew up, the places that helped make me who I am. For my first four years we lived in Varina, population 250. I don't remember much from those days, but I can picture the parsonage where we lived as my dad ministered to his first congregation. Our small, wooden Methodist church sat beside Varina's only other landmarks: a post office, a combination gas station/ general store, and a corn silo. There was no traffic, so I played in our front yard with my brother, doing what three- and four-year-old kids do, as well as spending many hours in the sandbox out back. Occasionally I would cross the street to visit an elderly lady I called Grandma and collect the cookies she liked to give me. If I broke my mother's rules I'd hear her holler out "LAW-RENCE!" the signal that I was in trouble. My punishment was to walk to the rear of the parsonage and sit on a nail keg to "think it over." My brother loves to tell that I made so many trips there that I wore a path in the grass from the front of the house to the back.

I have more vivid memories of Dayton, a town of 750 where we moved when I was in first grade. Behind the Dayton parsonage was a large, open field that sloped downhill to a creek (or as we'd say it, *crick*). It was my own playground, a place where the only rules were mine. Out there, I was the greatest cowboy this side of Roy Rodgers and Gene Autry, always the hero in my imaginary gunfights. A rope hung from a tree next to the creek, and I would use it to swing to the opposite bank to save a cowgirl in distress. I never got bored. They say the brain develops the most up to age seven, and I believe that playing by myself for hours on end stimulated my creative side, which was a big help in my career. My design of implants for hip and knee replacements, my operative technique, and my devotion to research are all products of my creative mind. And, of course, everything came together in Operation Walk, which may be the most significant creation of all.

I never knew when I was young how much my Dad struggled to support our family. My mom told me many years after he died that he went to the bank almost every month to get enough money to help us make it from one church paycheck to the next, but I never felt poor. I don't think my mom did either, but she wanted to be sure we knew what true poverty was like, so she decided to show us. One night at supper she said we were going to eat as if we lived in China so we would better understand the people who lived there. I looked down at my plate, shocked to see just a few dabs of food. I was a growing boy with a high metabolism so I was really hungry after that meal. An hour later I snuck down to the basement, where I knew there was a bushel basket full of apples. I left the light off and tiptoed, but somehow my mom outguessed me and halfway down the stairs I heard a loud "LAW-RENCE!" She didn't have to say another word. I was caught in the act. I turned around, climbed back up the stairs, and slunk past her as the door to the basement closed behind me.

All of this came back to me as I stood off to the side of a stage in Washington, D.C., in February of 2005. In a few minutes, the annual meeting of the American Academy of Orthopaedic Surgeons would officially name me its humanitarian of the year. But as a video played, displaying the accomplishments of Operation Walk, I was far away, reliving that night in Iowa when my mother tried to starve me. I suppose it was my brain's way of reminding me that I dedicated myself to helping the poor because of the way my parents brought me up. That memory also reminded me of my mother's message to be grateful for my blessings. She certainly would've told me to be humble in accepting the recognition of my peers.

Someone called me to the center of the stage, handing me an award and a check for $5,000 that would go to Op Walk. I set the glass statue down on the podium and stood staring out through the glare of the stage lights, unable to see Marilyn or my family and friends. I knew Chit Ranawat was in the audience, as was my good friend John Callaghan, who sat in the Lawrence and Marilyn Dorr Chair in Orthopedics at the University of Iowa. My colleagues, fellows, and work family were there too, so many of the important people in my life.

I would tell this audience that Operation Walk did not change the world, but it did change the world of our patients, who live in places where the disabled are discarded. We came bringing treatments that they would never otherwise receive, and for them, we sometimes seemed like a miracle that dropped out of the sky—an unexpected blessing that came as the answer to many prayers. We helped make bodies whole, which in the eyes of their communities made our patients worthy of respect again, worthy of jobs and mates and independence, worthy of belonging. We brought the gift of mobility, and for that, the recipients could not restrain their gratitude. Cicero said that gratitude is the greatest of all virtues, and it was not just a virtue of the patients. Operation Walk team members were restored by these patients, who would trust their lives to us, strangers from a foreign country who often were unable to converse with them, and who would leave them once our work was done. This profound level of trust touched the medical professionals who joined us and rekindled the dreams dreamt when they toiled to get their degrees and envisioned medicine as a human-to-human exchange instead of an impersonal transaction.

The sense of empathy, humanity, and gratitude that fills Operation Walk was seeded in me by my mother as my stomach growled on that winter night many years before. The concrete lesson in hunger seemed stupid to me as a fifth grader, but it stayed at the front of my mind as I was being honored. I hoped that the people in the room, especially those who were new to Op Walk, could feel that essence coming through.

# The Ultimate Goal:
# Giving Back Better than You Got

As I reflected on the past, I realized I was also speaking to the future, and I was drawn to another group in the audience, an incoming class of young surgeons being inducted into the orthopedic academy, so I directed the rest of my remarks to them. I wanted them to understand Operation Walk in the context of their own professional lives, which were just beginning.

I told them that there are four stages in the career of a doctor that they'd have to navigate to be happy. The first is the "Thrill of Victory," which comes with acceptance to medical school and continues through all the years of training as new surgeons anticipate the contribution they will make to society and to the lives they will improve and save. The thrill of doing good appears, disappears, and re-emerges throughout our careers, and it's especially powerful when patients come bearing gifts of thanks for the treatment they've received.

The second stage—I call it the "Agony of Defeat"—is the critical stage for success. Young doctors in training learn that complications can arise when they treat patients, but they expect to be the exceptions to the rule, the ones for whom nothing will go wrong. So when the first devastating complication occurs, they can temporarily lose all confidence. It's common for the first complication to be compounded by a second, a third, and even a fourth. Such a pileup of difficulties and unexpected results can put a doctor's confidence in real jeopardy. This is the moment of truth because doctors must choose between making decisions to avoid "losing" or making decisions to win. Once they assess the problem, will they continue to believe in themselves or continually second-guess? Will they trust what they know and let their intuition and experience guide them toward the best solution, or will they freeze or shy away from difficulty? Will they learn from failure and grow, or will they, on some level, give up? Medicine is stressful, and for a surgeon, each operation presents a new source of stress. If surgeons are afraid of a complication with each operation instead of having confidence of success, their risk of an inferior result grows. Burnout is prevalent in orthopedics, and this is the stage that creates it.

The third stage revolves around the realization that "There Is a God but It Is Not Me," and the sooner a doctor understands this, the sooner he or she becomes a true physician, a person concerned not just with fixing a problem but with healing the person who's experiencing it. In medical school, students are inundated with science and technology, but their teachers spend little if any time on the art of medicine—the building of a human connection between doctor and patient that elevates both. It's the art of finding a balance that keeps the doctor confident but also humble and able to offer love, and allows the patient to believe in a good outcome and appreciate the healing that comes, without expecting magic.

I can remember a time during my training when I thought I did not need to worry about patients liking me because they were going to be lucky to have someone treating them who was trained as well as I. Today I despair when I see that some doctors continue to believe that throughout their practice years. A doctor practices only scientific medicine, but a *physician* instills confidence with caring and kindness. I have come to believe those qualities are fifty percent of any successful treatment, which is why I've emphasized them in my practice and put them at the core of Operation Walk. I've lost count of the times I've performed operations that have not gone as I hoped, yet found that the patient was thrilled with the result, or so appreciated the improvement in their condition that they never complained. To me, this felt like a form of acceptance and forgiveness that came only because I was human with them and they knew I cared and had done my best. Realizing that the doctor is not a god, and understanding that healing can come from improvement in function and lessening of pain even if there is no "perfection," is a key for both patients and doctors. Appreciating that opens both sides to giving and receiving healing in ways that cannot come when we see surgery strictly as a means of repairing the "machine" of the body. How often I have seen the bodies and spirits restored by love, kindness, gratitude and belief in each other. When those are present, there's a grace that comes through us—a gift we are blessed to receive.

What has all this to do with Operation Walk? Once a doctor has matured through these stages and become a physician, a fourth stage comes to the fore: "Give Back Better than You Took." Most doctors have given their body and soul to their profession, and if they are fortunate, they've been rewarded with a good economic life and respect for their skills. When we've received a great deal, it's our responsibility to return to our profession and society some of the knowledge, techniques, and money we've accumulated. And as we do that, our gratitude for the blessings of life and of a career in medicine blossom.

When we move into this part of our careers, we have the insight that success is not defined by the destination we reach but instead by how we live and what we give to others. Helping people, improving their lives, being available at times of need are the mileposts of a doctor's journey. Sometimes the road is rough and we fall short or fail. We face pressures from the institutions we work for, we lose patients or can't help them as we'd like to, and we let our lives fall out of balance, but if we face the difficulties and find our way through them, I told those new surgeons, we emerge with more skill and empathy to give. If we give up, there will be no successful destination. Only if we *give back* in deeds and gifts will those who follow us respect our journey.

We give back in many ways, devoting more time to teaching, doing research or working in clinics for the poor. I've done all of these, and for me, there's no question that the most life-changing of them all has been Operation Walk.

Participating in an Op Walk mission gives us back our passion and reminds us of the good that can come from the hardships we have to face to achieve excellence. What we all bring home with us is the desire to keep experiencing the joy and satisfaction that come from freely helping those who need us the most. We're hooked on it and then we want to "pass the glory on" to others, which we do by our work and example.

## The Moment That Became the Tipping Point

As I finished speaking, I was grateful that in honoring me, the orthopedic academy was focusing a bright spotlight on Operation Walk and let me tell our story to so many of our 30,000 members and the vendors who work with them. The impact was enormous. We went into the ceremony with three chapters going on missions—Los Angeles, Indiana, and Denver—but soon surgeons across the continent were asking to work with us and founding chapters of their own. I think Malcolm Gladwell's book *The Tipping Point* has as good an explanation for what happened as any I can come up with. Ideas stay small, he says, unless three elements combine to give them the critical mass that tips them into snowballing success. First, they need the support of people he called *connectors*, vivid personalities who amplify and spread the word. In orthopedics, the surgeon-leaders of the first three Op Walk chapters fit the bill. Bring connectors like us into the room and soon we're matchmaking and facilitating, drawing in everyone around us. Second, an idea needs to be "sticky," which means it's wrapped in an unforgettable message. For Operation Walk, stickiness came when people saw the video footage of our missions. It's impossible not to be moved by seeing the faces of those who struggled to make their way into our clinics and came out dancing. The stories we told couldn't help but be compelling—and importantly, they were planted in the right context. Op Walk depends on the commitment and talents of orthopedic surgeons, and there was no better context than our national convention, and within that, the award ceremony itself, which had all of us glowing with belief in the importance of what we do and the life-changing power of our work.

From 1997 until 2005, our initial three chapters of Operation Walk operated close to 200 patients a year with four mission trips, and in Los Angeles we operated ten to twelve patients more in December for our USA mission. Those numbers exploded between 2005 and 2010 as a new set of intrepid surgeons joined us. Aaron Hofmann started a new chapter in Salt Lake City. David Stulberg and Victoria Brander launched a team from Chicago. Gerard Engh gave us a base in Virginia, Tony Di Gioia planted our flag in Pittsburgh, and Tom Thornhill and Richard Scott did the same in Boston. Paul Khanuja, a Baltimore surgeon, and his wife Maria joined an El Salvador mission in 2007 and went home to found their own chapter. We reached into Canada when Bob Bourne and Cecil Rorabeck began launching annual missions from London, Ontario. We also got support from singular independent surgeons who went on multiple trips with us, doctors like Richard "Dickey" Jones, who serves on the boards of both the L.A. and the Utah chapters, and Miami-based Carlos Lavernia, who has joined us on more than twenty missions. While their names may not be familiar to you, they're extremely well known in our field and regularly appear on lists like "the top 70 hip and knee surgeons in America." They were and are some of the most gifted and successful surgeon/researcher/inventers in the world, and in gathering support for Operation Walk, they've become even more visible as leaders in their communities.

As new leaders joined us, our L.A. team made sure they could get up to speed quickly so all of us could benefit. We had always leveraged what we'd learned by making sure that each new team received training from us, but as the Op Walk network grew, Jeri and Mary Ellen became its formal nervous system, creating a whole "How to Op Walk" mentoring program that they took on the road. Once a surgeon let me know he or she wanted to form a team, Jeri and Mary Ellen scheduled a day to meet with them, their potential team leaders, and anyone who wanted to help build a local Op Walk from scratch. Our calm, candid veterans flew in for a five- to six-hour presentation that covered every element of a mission—how to choose team members and select a destination, how to set up a preliminary site visit and what to look for on the ground, and how to get nonprofit status by starting a 501c3. If that tower of details wasn't enough to make fledgling teams soberly consider whether they were truly committed, there was still more to come after lunch, like the nitty gritty of how to raise money for the trips, exactly how to request implant and supply donations and whom to approach for those things, how to ship the supplies and get them through customs, how to select patients, and how to set up the teaching component of the trip. They shared war stories, sized up the potential team, and offered up tips, contacts, and home phone numbers.

The ace we always had was that the surgeons who were inspired to build their own teams had gone out with Op Walk first and they'd come home with a well of enthusiasm and belief in the mission that was deep enough to help them persist through the inevitable headaches, frustrations, and shortfalls that come with mounting a trip. Their Op Walk experience had opened their eyes and hearts, and filled them with the passion it takes to inspire volunteers, donors, and participants on every level. Jeri and Mary Ellen were there to walk them through selecting their first site, and seasoned volunteers would always be with them on their team's test run to be available for advice, reassurance, and backup. We helped novice team leaders jump the hurdles of cargo not arriving, language barriers, and financial hiccups. And if all went well once their mission was completed, they were confident enough to go it alone.

Our basic framework is solid, but not rigid. We've seen astonishing innovation from new teams—new approaches, new ways of bringing efficiency to missions, new ways of strengthening bonds with the people we serve. Our mission remains the same, but it's been illuminating to see the multiple ways each team expresses that vision.

In late 2005, we took our first step toward becoming international when I invited Cecil Rorabeck, an old friend and collaborator from many a panel and discussion, to join us on a mission to Panama, where beyond the work we did, I like to think we impressed him with an unplanned bit of fanfare. Toward the end of what seemed to be a routine round of surgeries, Panama's president, Martín Torrijos, came to our hospital with First Lady Vivian Torrijos for a press conference with our team. The first lady returned the next day to visit each patient. Cecil went home pumped, and recruited his research partner, Bob Bourne, another surgical ace and pioneer, to form our first Canadian team in London, Ontario.

We set up a training trip to Guatemala that gave the London group its sea legs and let Bob get his first taste of the challenges a surgeon might face on one of our missions. Guatemala had only recently popped onto our radar.

A Houston-based orthopedic surgeon, Brian Parsley, had been working with a group called Faith in Practice, founded around the same time as Operation Walk, which took medical, surgical, and dental missions to the country. From the time he heard about Op Walk, Brian told us, he wanted us to bring total joint replacements to Antigua's poor. Stepping into one of Faith in Practice's established bases, the Hermano Pedro Hospital (Obras Sociales del Santo Hermano Pedro) in Antigua, would give us access to both the patients we needed and a guide who knew the environment well.

For me, the trip was unforgettable in part because of a highly unusual drama that unfolded as we were working on a young woman who had traveled all the way from Nicaragua to seek our help. She had juvenile rheumatoid arthritis, a disease that inhibits normal skeletal growth, so she had very small bones and the face and body of a young girl. The arthritis in her hips had left her in terrible pain, and we planned to operate both. The Canadians had received their implants, including the small size we intended to use for her, from the Smith and Nephew company. But as we planned for her surgery by studying her X-rays and overlaying templates of the hip implant's stem, we were disappointed to see that her femur bones were too small for even the smallest stems we had in the Smith and Nephew supply.

Fortunately, I had small stems stocked at my hospital in Los Angeles, and Marilyn was coming to Guatemala the next day, so I called her and she picked up two of them so we could do the operation. It was only when she tried to get through security at the airport that she realized how much those small, curved metal pieces look like pistols. She explained to the TSA officer that they were medical supplies for an operation on a special patient, but the TSA is paid to be skeptical, and I think it was only divine intervention that allowed her to be waved through. One of the officers manning the gate that day was a man who'd been a security officer at my hospital, and he knew me. (What were the chances?) He let Marilyn and her package go, and she arrived in Guatemala with the implants right on time. They were no longer in their sterile wrapping, but a session in the autoclave solved that.

The problem the autoclave couldn't solve was that even these small stems were too large, though we'd been sure they would fit. Midway through the operation, Bob Bourne found that the broach he was using to open up space for the implant did not fit the woman's tiny femur. If the broach didn't fit, neither would the stem. We'd been misled by the X-rays we'd used to plan the operation, which had magnified the image of the bones at a scale that was different from the implant templates we were using.

We knew we were in trouble, but Bob continued while I tried to find a solution. I scrubbed out of the operation and went into a nearby storage area with our biomed technician Matt Sandusky. We'd brought a high speed drill with an attached carbide bit that cut metal, and we used it to shorten the small stem by half, then shaved metal off the sides according to our estimates of the patient's size. The area filled with observers as people heard about our dilemma. Bob's first attempt to seat the modified stem failed because it was still too big for the bone, so we took it back and shaved off more metal, then sent it back to be sterilized so Bob could try fitting it again.

This time it slid into the femur, much to the relief of all. Matt ran the second stem to the hospital's machine shop and cut it to size there, which was much faster than using the high-speed burr. Now Bob could accomplish the second hip operation in his usual manner. Bob Bourne is a world-renowned surgeon who has performed thousands of operations and authored numerous classic scientific articles with Cecil Rorabeck. He is retired today, but he'll tell you that this bilateral hip operation in Guatemala is one of the most uniquely memorable and satisfying surgeries he's ever performed. For me, Bob's assistant, every detail remains fresh in my mind, and Marilyn is still proud that her courier service enabled the operation to happen. Our young patient was walking with two crutches, free of her terrible arthritic pain, when we made rounds that afternoon, and she went home to Nicaragua when the Canadian team returned to Ontario.

Bob, like Cecil, was hooked on Operation Walk, and the Canadian team has returned to Antigua to perform an average of seventy-five total hip and knee replacements every year since. The Hermano Pedro Hospital became one of our regular destinations, and other teams also frequented Antigua. When Faith in Practice raised money to remodel the operating rooms of this hospital, Operation Walk donated $10,000.

## A Winning Approach from Salt Lake

The Guatemala trip not only sparked an ongoing relationship between the Canadians and the hospital, it also gave us the first look at a new team concept that Aaron Hofmann, an accomplished Utah orthopedist, wanted to try out with a small group from Salt Lake City.

Aaron brought members of his operating room team with him and planned to work with them in one of the four O.R.'s throughout the mission. If they clicked smoothly in the new setting, he hoped they could make a collective return as the core of a new Salt Lake team. Typically in the past, we'd mixed and matched staff in the O.R. from the ranks of our volunteers, but this was an experiment in tapping the power of familiarity, and it worked. In fact, almost all future surgeons who wanted to start a team that did solo missions used the model of bringing their own O.R. personnel from home.

This was Aaron's first time in Central America, but he would become a regular traveler to this part of the world. He said he had wondered beforehand what motivated the generosity of the family that had sponsored this mission, Jean, Jay and Jondy Cohen, and why Jondy, a surgeon, and his wife Rocki were part of the team. Then he saw the desperation of the patients in clinic and the concrete way we could lift it, and he understood. He returned to Salt Lake City and immediately organized a mission.

"I begged my O.R. staff and some relatives including my nurse sister, Kirstie, to join on a great adventure," Aaron remembers. His mother wrote a cookbook to sell to raise money for the first trip.

The Salt Lake team's initial destination would be Sonsonate, El Salvador, whose former mayor was the brother of a doctor that Julio Raya, our anesthesiologist, had met playing golf. The doctor, Juan Arce, also had connections to the minister of health. That would give them powerful angels—and they'd need them to take on the challenges they'd face. Each week in early 2005, there were news stories about the violence in El Salvador. During the country's long civil war in the 1980s, hundreds of thousands of people had fled to Los Angeles, where many young refugees had been pulled into gangs and later carried gang culture back home. When Jeri and Mary Ellen flew down to scout the area for Aaron's team, security was a major concern, and they didn't find many choices for housing fifty people. The most acceptable hotel had bullet holes in the walls, and when they pulled back the covers on the prison-thin mattresses, there were flecks of what looked like blood on the sheets. Those, for better or worse, turned out not to be human—it was their first exposure to bedbugs. Pesticide went on the packing list. Those weren't the only quirks in the quarters. Heating water for a shower required touching a couple of live wires together, and putting soap back in its metal dish could produce a mild shock. A bug zapper in the room made noise all night, and at 5 a.m. a local rooster began its own inescapable wake-up shift. This would not be any kind of relaxing vacation for Aaron's team.

But Jeri remarked on the beauty of the hospital, which reminded her of a hacienda, she said, with its courtyard and burnt orange walls. And as always, she and Mary Ellen were touched by the needs of the patients. She helped arrange for armed guards to stand watch outside the hotel during the Salt Lake team's stay, and our security protocols for the trip involved remaining indoors when not at the hospital.

"The patients were the kindest and most grateful for our care," Aaron says. "No one complained about pain, not after living with their arthritis for years. The hospital was overcrowded, including a full T.B. ward—this was something I had only read about in medical school. But there they were, covered in mosquito netting to help isolate each patient."

On that inaugural trip, Aaron's team and the other Op Walk volunteers who joined them performed about seventy total joint replacements in five days, including one for a woman who found her way onto the roster with sheer persistence. Though she was not on the schedule, she came every day to sit in the waiting room in case there was a cancellation. Finally, an opening came, and she got her new joint on the last day. A second memorable patient traveled twenty miles by horseback from her mountain community and then caught a bus to Sonsonate, using money her family had raised for her ticket. It couldn't have been an easy journey for someone with severe joint damage, yet she arrived in time for her operation and three days later, she was home again, free of her longtime pain.

"At the end of the first trip we took a group photo with the staff and the patients still in the hospital," Aaron remembers. "There was not a dry eye as the patients sang to us and thanked us for coming. As it turned out, we were the ones blessed. On every trip we take, we are the lucky ones to use our skills to help the neediest people in the world."

Aaron became a leader and connector within Operation Walk, forming new teams and innovating to build our efficiency. He established strong relationships with the government of El Salvador, and built a storage shed next to the hospital so the Utah team could keep equipment in country to reduce cargo requirements and expense. A training program he started brings doctors from El Salvador to Salt Lake City for a month to learn more surgical techniques, and other teams have adopted this component to build relationships and directly improve local doctors' skills. In 2019 the American Association for Hip and Knee Surgeons, with 4,500 members, named him its humanitarian of the year.

I've been especially grateful for an aspect of Aaron's contribution to Op Walk that is intimately familiar to me because of the way I grew up: he has found a way to support our mission and our patients by what amounts to tithing.

It's the highest of compliments to say that in him, I find echoes of my father, who was paid those low church wages that kept us at poverty level, yet tithed every year from the money he was paid for weddings. That precious supplement to our income went to my mother, but not before he'd given the first ten percent to the church. I remember how Dad taught the kids in his congregation about tithing, calling them to the front of the sanctuary and sitting on the floor with them. He'd place an old wooden coffee grinder in front of him and use it to tell the story of Aunt Nan, who was struggling to raise five children as a single mother. Money was scarce, but Aunt Nan used the "storehouse" drawer in her grinder to set aside "God's tithe" from what they had. Then, every Sunday, she had her children take some money from the drawer to give to the collection plate. Even with tithing, and perhaps because of it, Dad would say, Nan's children had what they needed, and they grew up to be ministers and professors. I know Dad would be pleased by Aaron's version of "God's tithe." He's the founder of an implant company, Total Joint Orthopedics, and every year he donates implants to Operation Walk in an amount equal so ten percent of the implant inventory his company sells. In all of orthopedics, Aaron Hofmann's tithing is the only example I've seen of this level of giving, and we feel blessed and grateful to be able to help so many more people because of him.

Op Walk lights the desire to give in everyone it touches, however they can, to make lives better.

# CHAPTER 8:

## Vietnam: Healing Old Wounds, Building Bridges

...................................................................................

Over its lifetime, Operation Walk has been a vehicle for many kinds of healing. It's focused on the body, of course, and it has proven to be strong medicine for our hearts and spirits, but I've also been surprised to see that it's been a balm for old wounds between nations, something that's come not from words and politics but from the closeness that builds as our teams and patients reach beyond old fears, preconceptions, and hostilities to experience each other as fellow humans.

I felt this strongly in Vietnam, which Op Walk first visited in 2008. Before that trip, I still tended to think of Vietnam mostly in terms of the war in which so many of my generation lost friends. I was a young Navy surgeon in those years, and though I wasn't sent to battle, I saw and felt the costs. So many decades later, I didn't have animosities, but I didn't have a sense of closeness to the Vietnamese either, so when one of our internists, Dr. Andrew Fishmann, suggested that we go, I was happy to have a chance to build bridges with the people there. Andrew's wife, Dr. Kim Le, was from Vietnam, and her sister and brother-in-law, Ann and Vince Pham, became valued ambassadors for Operation Walk, translating for us and facilitating our first mission, as well as the many to come. Crucially, they knew a doctor in Ho Chi Minh City, formerly Saigon, who welcomed us to his hospital.

We recruited George Etheridge, one of our greatest supporters, to go on that first trip. George is a big-hearted philanthropist who is also the founder and president of Tampa-based Precision Orthopedics, which distributes high-tech medical devices and has been a liaison for implant donations from companies like Zimmer-Biomet. He introduced us to a Florida ortho-pedic surgeon named Phuc (pronounced Fu) Vo, who quickly joined the team, sharing his dramatic personal history and bringing us all closer to the strangers we hoped to help.

Vo had fled Vietnam with his two older brothers in 1975 at the close of the Vietnam War. He had grown up in Bình Tuy, a village in central Vietnam that was close to Chu-Lai, where the U.S. forces had set up a base. The village was patrolled by South Vietnamese and American troops during the day and controlled by North Vietnamese and Vietnamese Communist (VC) patrols at night, putting it in the crosshairs of military activity. Nearly half of the 200 people who lived there were killed, and while Vo didn't lose any of his immediate family, their home was destroyed by mortar fire.

As the fighting wore on, the family moved farther and farther south, and by the time U.S. forces withdrew from the country, they lived just out-side Saigon. As the city fell, Vo and two of his brothers, one an officer in the South Vietnamese special forces, escaped on a military barge, and Vo remembers the way the barge spilled over with refugees and how he and his brothers struggled to climb on with his brother's wife and two children, one a six-month-old girl. Fourteen-year-old Vo and his brothers passed the baby back and forth as they helped the family struggle onto the deck, watching as many others lost their grip and fell into the water.

Packed in so tightly they could only stand, the refugees floated down the river and into the South China Sea. They drifted for seven days before being rescued by a U.S. Navy ship, which transferred them to an aircraft carrier whose deck was filled with more refugees. They wound up in a camp in Guam, where they stayed for a month, and then were offered a chance to relocate to the U.S. They chose Eglin Air Force Base in the panhandle of Florida because the climate there seemed closest to what they knew.

Vo and one brother became doctors, and years later, so did the baby they had carried to a new life. For seventeen years they were unable to unite with the family they'd left behind—their parents and four more siblings, including a brother who'd served in the South Vietnamese army and had been held for a time in a concentration camp. Finally, in 1992, they'd been able to come together in the U.S.

Despite the trauma he'd experienced, Vo had longed to return to his home country. He had first planned to go thirteen years earlier with another medical mission, but his father had died shortly before that trip and he'd never made it. He was elated when George Etheridge invited him to join us. For the first time in thirty-three years, he would set foot on Vietnamese soil, and he'd do it as part of Operation Walk.

## Relieving Pain, Bringing Peace

As well as contributing his surgical skills to the team, Vo eased the way for the rest of us, both practically and emotionally. Some of us were apprehensive about how we'd be received in a country that had endured so much suffering in the war with the Americans and with countrymen they'd faced as enemies. A good number of our patients had fought in the war, but as they opened up to Vo, who speaks fluent Vietnamese, he was surprised to learn that for the most part, there were no hard feelings about the past. People only desired to live in peace, and, like our patients everywhere, to find relief from their pain.

We worked hard to provide that relief, operating sixty-one patients and replacing eighty-five joints total, more hips than knees. Need was widespread, but as in so many places, costly total joint replacements were not considered to be a priority in the medical system. Our base, the Hospital for Traumatology and Orthopaedics, was the only such specialty hospital serving a city of almost six million people. It was understaffed and overcrowded, with two patients to a bed and others sprawled on mats in the halls. Often doctors would double up as well, with surgeons sharing the same O.R. for two different operations.

A team from England, organized by a leading surgeon there named Derek McMinn, joined us on this trip, and in their team videos, they chronicled their shifting reactions to the conditions we found. The central courtyard was a construction site "with scaffolding in the center and rubble, patients lying on the floor because there weren't enough beds," says one of the nurses, "and I was quite horrified to start. But then we saw the operating theater and I just relaxed, because when you set foot in their theater, they had this regime where you took your shoes off and put on your clean shoes and everything just seemed to fit into place like they knew exactly what they were doing and how they were going to do it." And we did. Jeri and Mary Ellen had traveled ahead with Vince Pham, our translator and guide, and protocols were very much in place.

The hospital had agreed to care for our patients above their usual standard, allowing each of them to have their own bed, though there were still four to six people in each ward with minimal space between them. We surgeons had a little more room to move, with four operating rooms set aside for us so we could perform our surgeries simultaneously, but not on top of each other.

The doctors on the U.K. team were surprised by the high incidence of advanced arthritis in younger patients. "What that means," one doctor said, "is that these people are the workforce and they may have children who need to be looked after, they may be looking after their parents and because of their age, and they may even be looking after their grandparents." Our surgery on just one person would improve the lives of all of those in the larger circle—that "multiplier effect" we'd noticed from the very first Op Walk trip.

Our group stayed in the Park Hyatt Hotel, which was similar to those in the U.S., and we had breakfast each morning in the dining hall on the third floor, where picture windows framed views of the Saigon River. We'd watch the day coming to life, and at 6:30, we'd board our bus and ride through empty streets to the hospital, at work before the city, which would soon be thronged with motorbikes.

Julie Anderson, one of our nurses, remembers the high volume of patients at our clinic, including some who had traveled for days and then waited a week to be seen by us. Shepherding them each day was a Vietnamese woman who was not a patient or relative, but a volunteer who told us she had come to the hospital to help just to be part of the excitement. We found another unexpected volunteer among the patients in this group, a war amputee who needed to have his arthritic hip replaced. He had been an English translator for the American forces and was excited to use his English for the first time since the war to translate for us.

With so many operations to complete in the three and a half days of surgery, our pace was strenuous. At night some team members would skip dinner and go straight to their hotel rooms to rest. Being a tourist for a day would happen after the surgeries were finished.

For me, the surgeries and relentless pace seemed routine, and even the logistical snafus we faced seemed to prove that wherever you go, people—especially bureaucrats—are the same. Jeri and Mary Ellen got into Ho Chi Minh City a couple of days before the team to ensure that the cargo was out of customs and found that, as on so many trips, it was not. With the team's arrival fast approaching, they spent all day at the cargo carrier's office trying to figure out what was going on with our thousands of pounds of hospital equipment and patient care supplies.

"Vietnam, like most places, can screw around all day trying to come up with answers, then five minutes before closing time they have information for you, but 'nothing can be done now because it is too late, and you have to come back tomorrow,'" Jeri says. "Well, we don't have that kind of time, so sometimes I have to be a little forceful. It is a miracle that someone hasn't had to fish me out of jail somewhere for that! I waylaid a motorcycle so I could put Mary Ellen on the back and get her to the customs office before it closed. Once we got there, I would not let them close the doors on us. I just stood in the way, demanding our cargo be released.

"When they finally caved and said they would let us have it, they tried to sucker punch me with, 'But we can't let the big truck deliver it tonight because big trucks can't be on the street after 5 p.m.'" So Jeri demanded a police escort for the truck to get our supplies to the hospital.

"They took us to where the cargo was and started opening every box, very slowly, just to try to make us give up," she remembers, "but I wouldn't let the escort leave and told them that even if we had to open boxes until midnight, I was not going anywhere without our stuff. Poor Vince, trying to translate for me! I am sure he was embarrassed and figured he might go to jail—but at that point, with our team coming in the next day from so far away, I was determined."

Grit triumphed once again. When the team landed, we had all the tools and supplies we needed to be up and running on schedule.

As I watch the U.K. team's mission videos, I smile to see them experiencing the effects of their work as if for the first time because they could see the miracle of it through our patients' eyes. "To see the response on their faces and their families and cousins and relatives," said one awestruck doctor, "everybody was there to see the end results. The expressions they gave and the joy and hugs were mind-blowing, basically." I couldn't agree more. Motivated to do whatever was needed, every member of our team quietly went above and beyond our job descriptions. Generosity was the default mode. When a patient with two different leg lengths needed a shoe lift but couldn't afford one, Jeri and one of our L.A. nurses, Yolee Casagrande, gave the young woman money and loaded her into a cab, then told the driver to take her to a shoemaker who would fit her with modified shoes.

There were a number of happy surprises for Vo on this trip, which would be the first of many Op Walk missions to Vietnam for him. The director of the hospital approached him to ask if he was the same Phuc Vo who had sent him a letter discussing his plans to join a medical mission thirteen years earlier. He had kept Vo's letter, and pulled it out to show him. Vo also made it back to his old middle school, where a sculpture created by one of his teachers still stood, and he was able to meet with some of his cousins. Talking to his hometown newspaper in Florida when he returned, Vo said he'd come away from his trip to Vietnam with perspective, not nightmares. "I don't think I have a lot of unpleasant memories," he said. "I saw destruction. Is it a bad memory? I kind of accept it as part of my growth."

## When Generals Call

We had a warm reception when we returned to Ho Chi Minh City two years later in 2010 and operated another sixty joint replacements. For me, though, what stands out about the trip was not the time spent in the city but the time I spent away. During that mission, the lead surgeon at the 108 Military Central Hospital in Hanoi asked me to come talk to him about bringing Operation Walk there. He was a military general, and I was a guest in his country, so I answered his summons with a visit.

My first impression of Hanoi was uncomfortable. Coming in from the airport, I could see the devastation that remained from the war. Ruins still scarred the landscape decades later, a stark reminder of healing yet to come. The city itself reflected an earlier chapter of Vietnam's history, with architecture designed during France's rule of the country. The French Colonial Metropole Hotel where I stayed had been a magnet for celebrities since it opened in 1901, with a guest list that included Charlie Chaplin and Graham Greene, who wrote *The Quiet American* there. Joan Baez, the folk singer, had sought safety in the hotel bomb shelter in 1972. Now, after falling into disrepair, closing and reopening, the Metropole was a modern luxury hotel still filled with history, and maybe a few ghosts.

I couldn't visit the city without paying tribute to John McCain, the Arizona senator who had been captured by the North Vietnamese after they shot down his A-4 Skyhawk as he made a bombing run in 1967. McCain was pulled from his plane with two broken arms and a broken leg, as well as other injuries, and thrown into a cell in Hỏa Lò Prison, nicknamed the Hanoi Hilton. He was tortured there and held for more than five years. When I visited the site, I was surprised to see that the infamous prison was in an ordinary neighborhood, housed in a nondescript one-story concrete building.

One room had become a lobby where videos celebrated North Vietnam's victory in what's known there as the American War. Farther in were the dark, tiny rooms into which as many as a dozen men had been crammed. The concrete cell where McCain had sometimes been held in solitary was cramped, with barely any light.

I was still thinking about the prison and the suffering inflicted and endured there when I met with the doctors from Hospital 108 at the Metropole. All three of them were military officers, and they were all business. The general in charge emphasized to me that Hanoi was in charge of health care in Vietnam, and they wanted us to bring Operation Walk to their hospital. My sense of caution was high after that fresh reminder of the fierce enemies our countries had been during the war. I do not remember any smiles. Still, I knew the Chicago team was interested in coming to Vietnam and I wanted to be sure we were welcome in the country, so I agreed that we would come to Hanoi.

Despite my initial doubts and perhaps low expectations, we received a warm reception from the doctors and hospital when we traveled there eighteen months later in September 2011. As in China, the patients seemed a little withdrawn and "stand-offish" to me when we met them in the clinic, and I understood we'd have to earn their trust and let them warm up to us. I would have to warm up to our hosts—the generals—too, though I didn't realize that until later, when it happened.

## Gifts More Powerful Than Words

Hospital 108 had 900 beds and we did our work in three buildings, with the clinic in one, the operating rooms in a second, and the wards in a third. That meant we had to send our newly operated patients on a grueling trip from the recovery room to their faraway beds. A couple of pre-med students on our team had transport duty, rolling people on gurneys with no side rails and small, uneven wheels up a thirty-degree ramp, then across two to three blocks of broken concrete sidewalks and up yet another steep ramp. When they finally arrived, the rooms were so small that gurneys wouldn't fit, so four people had to lift the patients and carry them sideways to their beds. The trip rattled the patients in every way, and our nurses had to work on restoring their confidence in our care once they were settled safely and could rest.

The students, for their part, got a feel for what it takes to do your best for people under tough and physically exhausting conditions, which was exactly our intent. Marilyn and I had initiated something called the Dimensions program at Cornell College, my alma mater. We wanted to help healthcare majors look beyond their tight focus on the sciences and be sure they got training that emphasized the *art* of medicine, the human side of the field. On every Op Walk trip, we took two Dimensions students, giving them the experience of spending a week living the life of a healthcare worker, coming in close contact with patients and observing the workings of the operating room. What they experience on Op Walk missions makes a lasting impression, and all our Dimensions participants have gone into healthcare fields, with the pre-med students—even the ones who worked so hard on trips like this—going into medicine.

Our patients were usually in a room with at least three others, and as we'd seen everywhere else, everyone, no matter how reserved and anxious they'd been when we met them, began to smile and express their gratitude once they saw the others in the ward happy and walking soon after surgery. A turning point in my own feelings came on the second day of surgery, when the hospital's head surgeon, the general I had found to be so cold on our first meeting, stopped me to ask a question. Did I remember the elderly woman on whom I had performed a hip replacement the previous day?

"Of course," I replied.

She was from a village in the mountains outside Hanoi, the general said, a place where everyone hated the United States because they had suffered so much from our bombings throughout the war. I wondered where this was going. And then the general told me that the woman had declared to him that when she went home and her neighbors asked, "What happened to make you walk straight?" she would tell them that a doctor from the U.S. had flown to Hanoi and operated on her and made her better. With a trembling voice, the surgeon said that my operation on this woman had done more good for the relations between our countries than all the politicians who had visited Hanoi, because now the hearts of the villagers would soften toward Americans. Operation Walk had been a powerful ambassador for the United States once again.

When our final round of surgeries was complete, Hospital 108 hosted an elegant banquet for us, complete with a band and dancing. Jeri wore a dress she'd had made by one of the city's famously affordable tailors, and we watched and laughed as the head surgeon sang karaoke to her and took a turn spinning her across the dance floor. The setting was strange—we were celebrating in an underground bunker and our hosts were heavy smokers, so the air was hazy enough to give one of our nurses an asthma attack—but the mood was festive. We'd made it.

"It was mind-blowing," Jeri says looking back. "Forty years ago we were bombing these people and now we were working together and happy. All I could think is that if we treat them as friends, their attitude toward us changes and they want to be friends." We couldn't undo the past, but we could begin to close the distance between us. I thought again of Vo, who gave so much to help countrymen he had last seen as he ran for his life. The war was over. All of us could heal.

## A Common Warmth: the Vietnamese and the Irish

I'm always impressed by the unique bonds that develop between different Operation Walk teams and the parts of the world they visit. The Chicago team, founded by my longtime friend Dr. David Stulberg and his colleague Victoria Brander, has traveled to Ecuador and Brazil, but they've had a special affinity for Asia. Along with return trips to Nepal, including an emergency mission to Kathmandu following a devastating 7.8 earthquake there in 2015, and repeat visits to several locations in China, the Chicago chapter has taken six missions so far to Vietnam.

Dave and Vicky share a commitment not just to surgery but to total arthritis care, and in their Op Walk work, they focus on helping hospital teams—administrators as well as surgeons and physical therapists—ensure that they're building a solid foundation for effective rehabilitation and ongoing care of people with arthritis.

Dave was intrigued by the idea of going to Vietnam, because like me, he had uncomfortable memories of the Vietnam War, and he was eager to put a different, more positive face on the image of Americans. Joining us on our first Vietnam mission, he was moved to see the way we could cut through fear, politics, and decades' worth of distance to find that we were more alike than different. He carried his excitement to an orthopedics conference, where he met Dr. Derek Bennett of Galway Clinic, head of an Irish orthopedic group, and invited him to come see for himself.

It proved to be a fortuitous match. In 2015, Dr. Bennett brought twenty of his colleagues on the mission to Hospital 108. Like so many of us, he was consumed by a sense of urgency by the end of his first trip—the need to do *this* kind of healing again—and he went home to found the first European chapter of Operation Walk.

I was grateful once again to see Jeri and Mary Ellen swoop in to help channel the pure energy of "Yes! Let's join Operation Walk!" into the actual mechanics of starting and following through. Before the impulse can fade, they're there for the newly minted leaders, guiding, supporting and getting a first mission date on the calendar—the firm commitment that makes the project real. No one has to fly blind. The collective learning of decades is at the ready, cautions and counsel on every topic, freely shared. Witness the entries in "The Operation Walk How-To Book" that team leaders receive. Entries run from "Ambassador" to "Zip Ties" with such practical advice as:

- *Air Travel:* ...*Take note on when your flight arrives back in the States. If it is very late at night, sometimes it can be difficult to get through Customs.*
- *Anesthesia machine:* ...*It is good to take photographs of the machines and get closeups of the model and serial number. You can bring this back and*

*show it to your anesthesiologist. If they are unfamiliar with the machine, they can always look it up through the model and serial number online and perhaps get a manual for it.*

- **Cargo list**: *…Remind your team that they are roughing it! They are not going to have everything they are used to having. The items on Mary Ellen's master cargo list are most essential.*

- **Changing area:** *…No fraternizing or going to the restaurant or bar with scrub clothes on. People in other countries perceive this to be dirty and then if a patient gets an infection they are going to hold you responsible for it.*

- **Warehouse:** *You will need warehouse space…The warehouse should have a loading dock or a place where someone can pick up a pallet with a forklift and put it on a truck… A public storage locker is not a good idea because you cannot palletize your items unless you get the kind that is big with the roll up door…*

When I heard the Irish group's co-director and lead surgeon, David Cogley, marvel at how each mission would require shipping "half a hospital halfway around the world and halfway back again," I couldn't help thinking of the guides, lists and protocols invisibly woven into the works. New teams learn that these are what keeps a mission from unraveling—along with compassion, persistence, and colored tape for organizing boxes. They bring their own discoveries back, renewing our excitement with their stories and their passion for this work.

The Irish team's video of their 2019 trip is filled with beaming faces—on both the patients and the volunteers—and I was struck by the true and easy connection they made with the Vietnamese. From the beginning, Dave Stulberg had mentioned the Irish team's instantaneous ability to connect. Maybe their effortless camaraderie was due to their farming backgrounds or a recent history of violent strife with their countrymen, or maybe it was just because of the warmth they found in each other's smiles.

"It's very interesting that they seem to be very similar to Irish people in terms of cultural heritage, in terms of outlook on life, and from the very beginning we seem to have hit it off," one of the PTs said of his Vietnamese patients. A nurse said simply, "They're really kind and welcoming, and they're the best type of people I've met in this world so far."

It particularly warmed me to hear one of the Irish PTs reflect, "They're very strong people. They're happy whatever you ask them to do, whether it's exercises or walking—they're just willing to do it and so thankful for all the help they're getting. I got talking to this really pleasant lady. She's got a lovely smile, very gentle. I asked her was she still working, because a lot of these people are not working and she's a 63-year-old lady, and she took a big smile and said she was a farmer. My father was a farmer and I wondered if she was a cattle farmer. She said she was a rice farmer. She told me she had loads of rice that she could give me."

One of the patients treated by the Chicago mission that introduced the Irish to Vietnam is Tran Van Tien, a young man who's since become an Operation Walk ambassador, serving as a volunteer for visiting teams and telling his story to help raise awareness of Op Walk and boost fund-raising efforts for Vietnam missions. Tran had a form of arthritis called ankylosing spondylitis, which severely stiffens the spine and leg joints. He had lived for years without the hope of treatment. "The only thing I was able to do was lie in one place, a burden to my family," he recalls on a video documenting the Irish team's 2019 mission. "For seven years the only thing I could think about was that I was stuck there, waiting to die."

Tran was enterprising, and when his family bought him a laptop in 2011, his world expanded, at least a little. He learned Photoshop and film-making and opened a photo studio at his home to earn money. He even met a woman online and fell in love. But the barriers posed by his disability were constant and disheartening. His girlfriend's family strongly disapproved of him. Potential employers admired his skills, but wouldn't hire him. "Seeing the distress that my condition caused my friends and family caused me to think a lot about my own death and how it would have been a way of getting away from everything," he admits. But he pushed aside the idea of giving up because, "If I died, I would have let all of the people that I love down. They put so much effort into helping me all my life, I couldn't imagine it."

Relief finally came when he heard about Operation Walk and applied—in secret, guarding his hopes. Even when he found out that he'd been chosen for an assessment, he played down his excitement, not wanting to raise his family's expectations. "When I called my family after the surgery to let them know it all went well," he says on the video, "we all cried with happiness and relief."

Tran needed surgery on both hips and both knees to restore his mobility and freedom, and he got it from two different Op Walk missions. To hear him talk about the life he leads now is to know that he savors every day, every step. He and his wife have a young son and a new daughter who's just a toddler, and Tran, who has taken business courses since his surgeries, now confidently supports his family. "I never once imagined that I would be able to walk down the street holding my wife's hand or that we'd be able to ride together on her motorcycle," he says. "Now that I can walk, my family's happy, my wife is happy, my child is happy. It brings happiness to everyone."

## Imagining Peace, and Creating It

My experiences in Vietnam have made me realize that even people who held guns against each other can become genuinely close when they meet for humanitarian work and not for confrontation. To me, Op Walk's work there is a living example of the vision John Lennon described in "Imagine." From our first wary visit until now, we've created a microcosm of the world as one.

Our friend and colleague Phuc Vo has gone on to develop a working relationship with the Ho Chi Minh orthopedic surgeons. He concluded that he could have the greatest impact on the quality of medicine in Vietnam by helping educate its doctors, and he has supported three of them, including the chairman of a medical school, to come study with him in Florida and become more proficient with hip and knee replacement.

Vo took his seventh Operation Walk mission trip in 2018, his first with the new Operation Walk Florida, which he co-leads with Dr. Brian Palumbo and the group's president, our valued, longtime friend Dr. Kenneth Gustke. With twenty-seven U.S. volunteers and fifty more from within Vietnam, the team performed thirty-one total joint replacements in Dông-Tháp General Hospital, which serves three million people but had never offered a total joint replacement service. Vo's dream—and plan—is to keep taking Operation Walk back to Vietnam.

To me, Vo, one of our next generation leaders, embodies the heart and soul of Operation Walk—giving, building bridges, empowering our colleagues all over the world, and truly demonstrating the meaning of peace.

# CHAPTER 9:

# A New Continent,
# a World of New Challenges

..................................................................

People looking at the places we took Operation Walk to during our first fifteen years or so sometimes wondered at the parts of the world that weren't on our mission list. Why hadn't we gone to India or Africa, for example, where so many enormous and varied populations have extreme needs? For me and the L.A. team, it was mostly a matter of finding the right opportunity. What seemed like a solid invitation to work in India, for example, turned out to be a non-starter when we realized our potential hosts wanted to use Operation Walk for their own religious purposes. I've always trusted that if the time wasn't right for me to go, another Op Walk team would eventually take a small step into new territory and open the way. Indeed, Dr. Paul Khanuja, took his Op Walk Maryland team to Ludhiana in the Punjab state of India in 2011 and has been returning yearly since then to perform hundreds of hip and knee replacements for impoverished patients. Paul is Punjabi, a Sikh, and chief of the adult hip and knee replacement department at Johns Hopkins. I can't think of a better match.

Operation Walk's first trip to Africa didn't come until 2012, when I traveled with our L.A. team to Arusha Lutheran Medical Centre in Tanzania. We'd held off from going during the first decade of the 2000s because of concerns regarding AIDS, which was then the leading cause of death in sub-Saharan Africa, the epicenter of the global AIDs epidemic, but now drug treatments were more available, bringing rates down. Importantly for us, HIV tests were being used universally before surgery, which quieted our worries that our team members could be infected by a needle stick or an accident in the O.R.

The first site in East Africa Jeri and Mary Ellen had scouted was in Kenya, the home country of one of my international fellows, Aamer Malik, who urged us to go and lined up a hospital for us to visit. However, sometimes the potential drawbacks of a place are so apparent that you can easily see the writing on the wall. "Where you would expect to see no smoking signs in the hospital there were 'no corruption' signs," Jeri remembers. That was worrisome. Bribery and payoffs for special treatment were all too common, we learned. Would someone try to charge "access fees" for our free services? Would our cargo wind up in the hands of customs "pirates" as it had in Mexico? We could sense complex risks, and we didn't have the kind of angel there who would make us feel protected and help us dodge trouble. More than that, we didn't hear anyone aside from Aamer clamoring for us to come, so we took Kenya off the list and kept our ears open for another opportunity in the region.

It came in the form of an invitation from an Iowa orthopedic surgeon I knew, Dr. Steve Meyer of Sioux City. Right around the time I started Operation Walk, Steve went to Tanzania for the first time. Unable to ignore the need he saw there, he came home to help found Siouxland Tanzania Educational Medical Ministries, STEMM, whose first goal was to take medical teams to Tanzania once a year to train the country's orthopedic surgeons—there were just eight for the entire population. Steve performed the first total hip replacement in the country and then the first total knee replacement. His mission and vision grew. STEMM decided it was urgent to bring ongoing care to Tanzanian children left without parents by the AIDS crisis, so it built an orphanage to house fifty, as well as feeding 5,000 children every day.

I often think about the way Operation Walk not only brings out the best in people but also puts us in contact with some of the most remarkable humanitarians in the world, whom we often find working and providing other services in the areas we visit. These are people whose spirits I recognize, the religious and medical missionaries, the volunteers who are compelled to ask, "How can I help?" and who are fueled and transformed by spreading the gifts that are in their power to give.

Steve Meyer is a visionary, and his work in Africa is so significant that he was awarded the Humanitarian of the Year award by the American Academy of Orthopaedic Surgeons in 2020. Back in 2012, when he invited us to bring Operation Walk to his area and said he and his team would work alongside us, we didn't hesitate to go.

Steve introduced us to another person who was devoting this life to the wellbeing of the poor in Tanzania. Dr. Mark Jacobson is a Minnesota native who, like Steve, went to the country on a Christian medical mission and found his purpose in improving the health infrastructure there. Dr. Jacobson, educated at Harvard and Johns Hopkins, had worked for more than two decades at the Selian Lutheran Hospital in Arusha. He was now the administrator of the Arusha Lutheran Medical Center, a facility that would make an excellent base for Op Walk. All the key pieces seemed to be in place, and a pre-trip visit by Jeri and Mary Ellen confirmed that we'd have everything we needed. Although it would be an unusually expensive trip, with long hours in the air for the entire team and high cargo fees in addition to our usual hotels and meals, we were excited to go.

## Meeting the Maasai

The flight to Arusha went through Tanzania's former capital, Dar es Salaam, a port city on the Indian Ocean below the horn of Africa. From there, we flew east over the savannahs (grasslands) near Arusha, and we could see the famous flat top of Mt. Kilimanjaro, 19,000 feet high and the tallest mountain on the continent. Arusha itself was a busy, modern city of about 400,000, and the doctors who met with me expertly discussed the country's difficulties, especially the shortage of water. Much of the land surrounding Arusha is used for farming and grazing, and the area is home to the Maasai, semi-nomadic herders whose lives revolve around their cattle. They're some of the tallest people in the world, striking in their bright red or blue traditional dress. When we saw a crowd of Maasai chanting and marching along the road at the edge of town, we were told this was part of a ceremony. A boy was being led to his circumcision, a required step toward becoming a warrior—a protector of the tribe and its animals. We were fascinated, especially since we knew that many of our patients would be Maasai.

At the hospital, everyone we met was welcoming. The morning typically began with a meeting in a small amphitheater where the staff would talk about the plan for the day. That would be followed by prayers—this was a Lutheran hospital—and then by singing. One of Jeri and Mary Ellen's most vivid impressions on the pre-trip had been of walking in at the end of a meeting and being met by voices raised in song.

The Maasai have managed to live adjacent to modern technology without being engulfed by it, something we realized when we saw that many of our patients were unfamiliar with cellphones. One member of our team, Yancy Clark, delighted us all by taking photos and videos of our Arusha patients, who reacted with amazement, and sometimes fear, at seeing their images captured that way. But Yancy, who managed the patient X-rays in our practice at home, was known for his way of putting people at ease, and shock turned to laughter and a feeling of community. Yancy was thrilled to connect with his African roots, and we were glad he was with us. There was much tiring physical work to do, but I looked around and saw us having fun, which is the way I think it should be—even when we're pushing patients up and down three floors of ramps because the elevators aren't working. Our patients were extremely warm, cheering each other on and bravely allowing us to use our very foreign medical techniques on their bodies.

On both sides of the cultural exchange, all of us were seeing and experiencing the unfamiliar, like the older patient who had never been on the second story of a building and whose many wives came to the hospital to care for him. One of the first patients I operated was a tribal leader in his 60s. I was surprised to see that his tissue did not have good turgor, which is to say it was "mushy," more like what I'd expect to find in a ninety-year-old who had been sick for weeks, rather than in a healthy man like him. That was a great concern because in the short term, such tissue posed a higher risk of infection, and over time, its support for the implants would likely erode more rapidly. I learned what was behind this condition when Steve Meyer took me to a village an hour outside Arusha. We drove past agricultural fields whose crops were the village's main—but very small—source of income and arrived at an impoverished village where people lived in simple huts and houses, some with thatched roofs, most with open holes for windows.

At one home, we stopped to watch a man who prepared for a meal by picking up a hollow wooden tube with a sharp, pointed end and sticking it into the jugular vein of a cow standing in front of him. He let the blood drain into a gourd and gave it to his wife, who Steve said would add herbs and spices, making a drink for their dinner. This was a daily process, so the cows were rotated and only tapped for blood only every two weeks, which kept them healthy. The Maasai, I learned, subsist almost entirely on milk, meat and blood. I now understood the state of the tissue I was seeing in surgery. It had been infiltrated with bovine cells, enzymes and antibodies, which changed both its nature and structure.

Cows were central to the life of a village, which made them social currency. A common dowry gift was a cow, and if the groom were too poor to offer one to his bride's family, the wedding was off. Love only goes so far! Cows also determined the community hierarchy—the bigger the herd, the higher the status. My patient, the village leader, had an impressive nineteen head of cattle. When I made rounds after surgery, he was enthusiastic in his thanks and gestured energetically as he praised what we had done for him. His ultimate compliment was the declaration that I must visit him in his village, where he would gather everyone around a large fire and kill a steer that would become our banquet. That is one gift I am truly sorry I did not get to experience.

We only operated twenty-nine patients with thirty-two joint replacements, but we knew what it would mean for each of them to return home able to walk without pain, crucial for a people who traveled far on foot. We also helped open the door for future missions to the region by Op Walk teams, including the one Steve Meyer led to Arusha in 2014.

I credit our trip with firing up at least one next-generation humanitarian as well, Katie Callaghan, the daughter of my friend and fellow Iowan, Dr. John Callahan, an orthopedic surgeon who's an international leader in his specialty. To celebrate her college graduation, Katie had asked her dad to make the trip to Tanzania with her, and the experience helped cement her choice to become a doctor for the poor. She still remembers the pain of a Tanzanian woman in her thirties, "who could barely take one step onto the exam table in her pre-operative screen, yet had to squat to defecate daily because of her lack of indoor plumbing." Being there to see the woman walk freely again without pain was life-changing, Katie says, "a snapshot of the tremendous impact modern medicine can have in alleviating suffering, and further evidence to me of the privilege it is to get to be a part of this profession." Katie joined an Op Walk team that went to Havana when she was in her third year of medical school, and today she's launching her career with a focus on family medicine and helping meet the needs of underserved communities. Arusha is close enough to the Serengeti to be a popular departure point for safaris, and we couldn't leave Tanzania without getting a look at the legendary wildlife. A visit to Ngorongoro Crater National Park, a few hours out of Arusha, let us see animals I only knew from zoos and movies. A high point was being able to watch as a pride of lions took down and ate a wildebeest—nature in action. As they devoured their kill, we noticed jackals gathering at the periphery, first just one, then another and another until thirty minutes later there was a pack of twenty-five. The big cats seemed oblivious, but when a couple of the "observers" foolishly crept too close, one of the lions lifted her head, roared and gave chase, scattering the whole bunch.

Later on the trip we saw a gray rhinoceros, and while it was impressive, I was sad that we didn't see a rare white one because the residents studying under me in the 1990s had nicknamed me The White Rhino, which I take as a reference to my thick skin and way of charging in horn-first, without asking. John and Katie Callaghan made sure I didn't leave without a wooden white rhino, a souvenir that I still have today.

## Tanzania to Congo: WOGO

Two years after our trip to Arusha, another Op Walk team made its way there, a singular group built around a multi-city core of women surgeons who share leadership and handle the surgical duties on each of their missions. WOGO, Women Orthopaedist Global Outreach (whom I'll tell you about in more detail a little later on) joined Steve Meyer in 2014, first making a scouting trip with Jeri and Mary Ellen to get the lay of the land. It was only their third Op Walk mission.

Fifty-four patients crowded into the screening clinic when the full WOGO team arrived with tons of medical supplies and equipment, and over the course of three-plus O.R. days, they operated on thirty-two patients, replacing forty-four knees and treating four more patients who only needed injections.

"The deformities in Tanzania were probably the worst we've encountered," says WOGO co-founder Robyn Hakanson, something attributed to the high levels of fluoride in the area's water. We had passed along our experience with "mushy" tissue in the Maasai, and her team also noticed higher than usual amounts of bleeding in the patients.

Like all Operation Walk teams, WOGO only performs surgery on adults, but the team is committed to inspiring and helping women and children in other ways, and they traveled an hour out of town to visit Steve Meyer's STEMM Village, distributing shoes and school uniforms to the children there. More shoes went to kids at Glorious Orphanage and at The Plaster House, a residential program that supports children who are receiving and recovering from surgery to treat their disabilities.

WOGO followed their Arusha mission with one that took them to the other side of the continent, the city of Kinshasa in the Democratic Republic of the Congo, where they took a team of fifty into the Biamba Marie Mutombo Hospital. The undertaking was immense, with all the tricky logistics that go into assembling, shipping, claiming and setting up more than 9,000 pounds of equipment and materials, and then shipping home another 2,000 pounds of equipment at the end of the mission.

They were accompanied on the trip by former NBA star Dikembe Mutombo, who is a major philanthropist and hero in his homeland. His Mutombo Foundation was the leading funder of the hospital, named for his mother, and his presence stirred excitement everywhere. Unfortunately, even his support couldn't undo the difficulties of the trip. The hospital's lone sterilizer broke down and there were frantic calls and texts for advice as the team tried to formulate a new Plan B, hunting for a nearby hospital with working equipment that could assist. The team jury-rigged a system of sending tools across town for sterilization—but then that hospital's autoclave stopped working as well.

Surgery was shut down, and patients in the holding area for their procedures were sent home. It was the hardest mission WOGO had experienced, and team members struggled to get through their despair after the surgeries were cancelled. Some decided that such disappointment was more than they wanted to endure again, and this was their last mission. Others, like Robyn, were able to take a longer view. As far as they knew, they were performing the first total knee replacements in the country, and the successful outcome of the operations they'd completed would build trust. The hospital's medical personnel had a voracious hunger for everything the team had to teach and would keep using new protocols and techniques. They'd taken the first steps and there would be more.

I wish those who lost heart at the end of the mission could see what is so clear to me now: WOGO elevated the level of medicine at Mutombo Hospital the way the very first Operation Walk mission did in Cuba. The hospital made improvements after the team left, adding air conditioning, buying anesthesia machines that work, and adding a new sterilization system. A cardiovascular surgeon who wanted to begin performing surgery there thanked WOGO for exposing the weaknesses of the hospital.

It's not been possible yet for the team to return. Intermittent Ebola outbreaks and political instability have prevented that to date. But Robyn vows they will. "We have to come back," she says. "There are so many patients we have to help."

## The Ghana Connection

Operation Walk's strongest and most lasting connection on the continent came in 2016, when the Syracuse group—founded in 2011 by orthopedic surgeon brothers Seth and Brett Greenky and their operations director Kimberly Murray—took a team of twenty-five to St. Joseph's Orthopaedic Hospital in Koforidua, Ghana.

Before heading to West Africa, the Syracuse team had trained with us and followed our now-familiar path into Nepal, Panama, and Guatemala to become active and integral members of the Op Walk family, coming from the smallest city in the Operation Walk network. The Syracuse doctors are talented and confident, but Ghana tested them with challenges unlike any we'd seen, and I stand in admiration of the way the group has steadily found ways to adapt and innovate on its five missions there.

Kim Murray set out for the country to follow up on a request I'd gotten for Op Walk's help. We didn't have anything as specific as an invitation from a hospital, so she flew into Accra, the sprawling modern capital on the Atlantic Coast, and walked in "rather cold" as she puts it, with just a couple of connections there. Through the Child Malnutrition Foundation, a nonprofit linked to a soymilk producer called Vitamilk, she met a former Ghanaian minister of health, and with him she spent several days searching for a possible base. The city has a population of more than two million, and "it was like looking for a needle in a haystack to find a place where we could work," she says. "We went to seven or eight hospitals, but we have very specific needs. We need access to their people, we need a place that will give us four O.R.'s for a week, plus a sufficient size ward." At stop after stop, that was too much to ask.

Just when they were ready to give up, someone suggested that they look at a couple of other areas beyond the city. Two hours outside Accra they got lucky. "By chance we drove to Koforidua and found a hospital there that is orthopedic only. I took a tour and it was the perfect place," Kim says. "They were willing to stop elective surgery to let us use their O.R.'s. They had the right number of beds and leadership that was enthusiastic about our coming. At the very last minute we had a viable option."

St. Joseph's was founded by the Brothers of St. Joseph of Holland, and though its facilities were simple and the patients were housed in open-air wards like the ones we'd seen in other locations near the equator, it did have a couple of welcome modern features: air conditioning in the O.R.'s (but only in the O.R.'s) and startlingly good sterilization equipment. "That was a blessing for us," Kim says. "The Brothers got someone to donate state-of-the-art autoclaves and sterilizers. Central sterile looked like it had been dropped in from someplace else—it was the best of any country I've been to for Op Walk."

## Sickle Cell Disease, and Bones as Hard as Stone

Kim and the Syracuse team began planning for the trip, and when they started getting X-rays of potential patients and tracing medical histories, the first thing that jumped out at them was that they'd need to know more about sickle cell disease. "Really unique to Ghana is the tremendous number of people who are sickle cell positive," Kim says, "and that's the genesis of a lot of their problems"—including the dominant bone conditions the team would see and treat.

Sickle cell is a disease of the red blood cells, which carry oxygen through the body. When they're healthy, the cells are round and smooth and travel easily through the small blood vessels, but altered by the disease they become hard, sticky, and C-shaped (like a farmer's sickle, thus the name). The diseased cells die early, leaving people anemic, and they get stuck in the blood vessels, cutting off the oxygen supply to the tissues. One of the first spots in the body to become oxygen-depleted is the hip area, and when that happens, bone cells in the head of the femur die. That's called avascular necrosis, AVN. The dead bone collapses under its cartilage and becomes misshapen, and without support, the cartilage shears away. Disabling arthritis and pain result in the ravaged joint. This is what the Syracuse team saw in the vast majority of patients as they began their first Op Walk screening clinic. On a typical Op Walk mission we treat many older patients because osteoarthritis is a disease of the old, but in Koforidua, the clinic was full of severely disabled people in their 30s and 40s, and as young as 17.

"Sickle cell goes uncontrolled in Ghana," Kim says. "They don't have the resources to manage it as you would in the U.S. so it progresses very quickly. Of the patients we've seen over the five times we've gone, I'd say two-thirds to three-fourths are sickle cell positive, meaning they have sickle cell trait and the disease could erupt at any time, or they have the disease itself."

The reason for this is fascinating. People with the sickle cell gene don't get malaria, so natural selection looks on it as a positive trait and allows it to be passed on. It's a tough genetic trade-off—"Either you have sickle cell or malaria there," Kim says, and though it's treatable, malaria is Ghana's leading cause of death.

Though the Syracuse team was alert to the presence of sickle cell, it wasn't prepared for one of its effects: it makes bone tissue extremely hard. Writing on the team's blog in 2018, one of the surgeons describes the way he struggled to adapt to what felt like a strange new reality, where hammers and saw blades are suddenly no match for the bones they're trying to shape. I'd like to quote him at length because he provides a clear and unforgettable description of the disorienting world the surgeons were thrown into when they got to Koforidua.

"In the course of your life, you have learned the concept of force modulation," he writes. "Through a process of trial and error, you have learned how hard to close a car door, how gently to open a sugar packet, how carefully to hammer in a nail, and how cautiously to pass a thread through the eye of a needle. It takes practice, practice you sometimes don't even realize you're doing, but anyone who has successfully obtained toothpaste from a tube knows what I'm talking about.

"In orthopedics, we learn the same concept," he continues. "Through a rigorous and well-governed training process, we learn how hard you can pound a hip stem into a femur, or how tightly you can turn a screw into bone. Sometimes—and this is a universal truth—we learn things the hard way. We learn to do it right by doing it wrong, but learn it, we do.

"But imagine if you suddenly found yourself in a world where those rules of force modulation were suddenly inapplicable. You push a car door shut and it barely moves. You go to open a bag of salt & vinegar potato chips, and it doesn't open. So you pull as hard as you can AND IT STILL DOESN'T OPEN. Wait... what? This is joint replacement surgery in Ghana. The bone we have learned to handle so carefully in the States is as hard as granite here... We deplete batteries and wear down metal saw blades just trying to cut through their bones."

Because of this, the surgeons had to relearn the basics they took for granted and find ways to handle the complexities of bones affected by sickle cell. "The bones are hard, but also brittle," Dr. John Parker, another member of the surgical team, explained in a 2019 blog entry. "They don't budge... until they break... For joint-replacement surgeons, the net effect is comparable to driving a car in a big blizzard or snowfall: the actions and input feel familiar but can result in wildly different outcomes in a single moment, and sometimes without any warning and somehow, it always surprises you."

## Recalibrating in Real Time

Heading into this "blizzard" the first time, the team had to stop and regroup, knowing it was going to have to learn as it went, Kim says. "When you do screening clinic, you're mapping out patients for four days of surgery, but we were thrown a curve ball. We circled the team in to say, 'We committed to this many patients, but it's going to take a lot longer than we thought. Do you want to take people off the schedule or go ahead?' And the team overwhelmingly said, 'We'll stay as long as it takes.' Our surgeons are fast, and in other countries, we're usually out of the hospital by 5:00 or 6 at the latest, but here we never left until 10, 11, 12... We felt like we honored our commitment, and to do it we needed the whole team to agree. It was difficult, but after that first time, we could course-correct and re-direct. We brought additional people so we could do shifts in pre- and post-op. The surgeons didn't care, but we but have to be sensitive to the rest of the team's needs. We're in an environment where it's 90-plus degrees with very high humidity." And team members, too, must rest.

The easiest cases the team sees in Koforidua, surgeon John Parker says, are akin to the hardest ones they'll generally see at home. It's not just joints affected by sickle cell, but also untreated trauma of the sort we so often see in missions across the world, where injuries caused by a scooter accident or a fall or cement blocks of a wall landing on top of a leg can go unrepaired for years.

One typical Koforidua patient was a twenty-two-year-old with a dislocated right hip from a car accident, whose right leg was ten centimeters shorter than his left. Asked how long ago his injury occurred, he replied "seven years." Then there was a smiling young woman on crutches who had serious arthritic deformities in each hip that she said she'd had for many years, though she was just twenty-one.

The team had to proceed with extreme caution, as sickle cell can produce clotting crises that threaten people's lives, and stress—like the stress of undergoing an operation—can bring on a clotting crisis. Along with everything else, they had to come up with a sickle cell protocol for minimizing the danger.

Reflecting the very best of Operation Walk, the Syracuse team found its balance and produced solutions for patients like these from the first difficult day, even as it coped with rolling blackouts and learned to communicate with people who spoke English but needed English-to-English translators to be understood through their distinctive accents and dialects. Through it all, every member of the team, says Kim, was overwhelmed by the warmth of the patients.

"The Ghanaian people are wonderful. Certainly in some parts of the world we've gone people are scared and there's a trust issue, a reserved eagerness with doubt about what we can do, but the Ghanaian people were the most welcoming, open, and warm people I've ever met. From day one they welcome you, embrace you, and they trust you. It's such a different feeling from other places we've gone to. Their gratitude, their genuineness, their purity—they're very spiritual people," Kim says.

"Ghana is one of highest mission-impacted places in Africa. On the plane over, we were surrounded by religious groups on their way to provide help, not just with healthcare but help with sustainability—managing little businesses, teaching their children. Walking through Accra you get a sense of the impact of Christian missionary work. You might see something like the Spirit of Jesus Lube and Tire shop, or the Mother Mary corner convenience store. It's a very spiritual and overwhelmingly Christian country."

Yet the help that arrives, including what Op Walk brings, is dwarfed by the scale of the need. "We try to limit the patients we screen to a reasonable number," Kim says, "but despite that, each year they send 350 to 500 cases to us before we go. It's heartbreaking. Out of those, probably ninety-five percent do need surgery, so over the course of years we've had to put internal criteria in place. Last trip it was age-based, and we only did people under forty. Certainly there are a lot of older patients who need care, but we tried to do the greatest good to have biggest impact. If a person is working or going to school, we can help them be self-sustaining." And those people that are helped sustain others as well.

Left to her own devices, she might put other filters in place. "When I'm in the screening clinic, I always have a baby in my hands, and my joke among the doctors is that I get to have veto power if I find a lady with a baby, and move her to the top of the list." It's hard for her—as for all of us in Operation Walk—to bear responsibility for deciding who's most deserving.

"What we are doing is just a drop in the bucket," Kim says. "That's what's difficult. We've had to put crowd control in place when we come to do screenings. People come to the hospital because there's that glimmer of hope that they can get the surgery. It's an emotionally overwhelming trip for me. People will see you in a hallway and pull on your lab coat. 'Can't you please help my sister or mother?'"

The gratitude the team receives is also overwhelming, Kim says. "There's not a year we've gone back that people don't travel in to see us. One woman spent nine hours on a train with a baby, just under two, and walked all the way back to tell us how grateful she was and how we changed their life."

# Small 'Stone,' Enormous Ripple

Hundreds of patients have now benefited from the work of these Syracuse all-stars, and it all began with the tenacity and resilience that got them through their first difficult mission, where against all obstacles, they were able to directly change the lives of forty-six people. Every team on every mission longs to do more, but looking back at the exhaustion and exhilaration of that first trip, Dr. Parker found a perspective I can't help but agree with:

"A stone thrown into a still pond creates a ripple that propagates in every direction," he wrote. "And the stone that these Op Walk people have thrown… I think it's entirely possible that its ripple will spread through Ghana, and even Western Africa, and help change the way the population thinks about health care. Maybe the people of Op Walk touched more than 46 people. Maybe they touched millions."

From all I've seen since Operation Walk began, I can't help but believe that this is true.

# CHAPTER 10:

## Roots and Branches:
## Operation Walk's Tree of Life

..........................................................................................

In the spring of 2019, I returned to Cuba for the fifth time to the CIMEQ hospital with our L.A. team. Since our first anxious trip there, Cuba had become a regular destination for many Op Walk missions, and a brand new group from Albany would follow us there in the fall. When our whirlwind of work was done—fifty patients with fifty-eight joints replaced—Jeri, Mary Ellen, and I walked to the park across the street with our host and friend Dr. Alfredo Ceballos. Twenty-two years earlier, to celebrate the success of our inaugural Operation Walk adventure, we'd planted a scrawny sapling in that park. Now, we carried another sprig of a tree to put in the ground beside it, this one to mark the long and close friendship we'd developed with so many at this hospital.

As we neared the park, I was stunned to see the spreading branches of a tall golden oak that shaded the spot where we had once patted the soil around a bare twig, not quite sure it would survive. It was a thrill to stand with the same people who did that first hopeful planting and take in the surprising strength and beauty of what had risen. For me, nothing could ever symbolize the growth of Operation Walk better than that tree. I never expected either of them to thrive the way they have, and it's been the pride of my life to see Op Walk spread its reach to help so many thousands of people.

Jeri and Mary Ellen turned our experience into a template and support structure that would let new groups build missions more easily from the ground up, train with us and then take off on their own, using the Op Walk model as a starting point for taking caring, compassion, and better medicine around the world. By following their own passions and inspired ideas for better ways to help, they've brought depth and richness to Operation Walk in ways that have surprised and inspired me. You could say that each Op Walk chapter has an inner fire carried from the original Op Walk flame, and each team's distinct vision is alight with generosity, resourcefulness, and medical ambition that's expressed in many forms.

As I read their trip logs, view the videos that document their missions, and have the chance to meet and work alongside the exceptional people who are continually pumping Op Walk full of life, I feel blessed to see our work spiraling out into the future, carried farther by each new Op Walk team. Operation Walk is here for the long haul, evolving and adapting in front of our eyes. When Covid-19 brought limitations on travel, some groups turned their eyes back to the U.S., imagining ways to strengthen our surgical and arthritis-care efforts here. Every obstacle and victory is a teacher.

Each of our teams deserves its own book filled with its own unforgettable stories of healing, discovery, and connection with the purest form of medicine, the kind rooted in love. I can't begin to do them all justice, so I'd like to spotlight just three groups you've seen glimpses of already: WOGO, Operation Walk Denver, and Op Walk Canada. They've enriched our idea of what Op Walk can be, and their passion is helping to ensure that our work will continue to flourish. As Operation Walk becomes a marathon, it is also a relay, with each of us passing the essence of this mission to the next willing person, always with a true sense of wonder at how much we can do, one generous act at a time.

## WOGO: What Happens When Women Take the Lead

For me one of the most exciting developments of Operation Walk came in 2009, with the formation of WOGO, Women Orthopaedist Global Outreach.

Created by a high-powered group of women surgeons, WOGO saw a need that spoke loudly to them—the wellbeing of women and girls in impoverished nations—and built a web of partnerships to help meet it.

As Robyn Hakanson tells it, the WOGO story has a classic set-up: "Five women walk into a bar…"

"Seriously," she says, "that's actually how it started—five of us in an airport bar."

Robyn, who's based in Salem, Virginia, and the other four doctors—Rinelda Horton, from Gaithersburg, Maryland; Audrey Tsao, based in the D.C. area; Jennifer Cook, based in Trinity, Florida; and Ginger Holt, of Nashville—had all attended a medical conference and been part of a panel on the impact of arthritis on women. As they prepared to fly off in different directions, they sat talking over drinks. Ginger described an experience she'd had on an Op Walk trip during her medical training and a wild notion took hold. What if they all went—together? Women are a rarity in this field—only four percent of the orthopedic surgeons in the U.S. are female—and here were five of the proud few, seated at one table. What if they joined forces to increase their impact in the world by launching an Op Walk team whose leaders and surgeons were all women?

Spread out across the country and facing demanding schedules in the O.R. as well as juggling research, teaching, families and the avalanche of demands that filled their normal lives, it took them two years to create a formal plan and approach Zimmer Biomet, the implant company, for support. It took another year for them to make their first trip, to Kathmandu, a trial by fire that Jeri helped ensure they'd pass, giving them the confidence to continue. What was crystal clear from the beginning was WOGO's call to help women in impoverished areas, who are disproportionately impacted by arthritis. As a rural woman labors and cares for her family, her average work day can extend to almost twelve hours, making her a likely candidate for arthritis and other joint problems. Unfortunately, in many parts of the world, though women's needs are great, their access to care is restricted simply because their cultures don't value them as much they value men. WOGO wanted to help change that.

"Our plan was to follow the model Op Walk established for surgery and education with one exception," Robyn says. "We decided to do just knees because we felt that doing just one type of surgery would minimize inventory and streamline things like PT and make it easier for everyone. However, we also knew that we were WOGO, and wanted to do our own outreach into communities. We weren't sure at first what that would look like, but on every trip, we've found the perfect opportunity to make our mark." Improving the everyday lives of women and girls is "something that is every bit as important to us and our volunteers as the surgical side of things," Robyn says, "and the outreach opportunities always seem to find us."

## Gifts for the Girls of Kathmandu

On the scouting trip for that first Nepal mission in 2010, Jennifer Cook had her purse stolen, and while she was waiting at the U.S. Embassy to have her passport replaced, she fortuitously met the founder of a group called the Little Sisters Fund. "Basically," says Robyn, "the mission of this group is to make sure that girls get to go to school too—not just their brothers. When we returned for our trip in September, we met with the girls and spent time with them." In a video clip of the meeting, Robyn and Jennifer sit at the end of a long wooden table that's lined by little girls in blue school uniforms and plaid ties, their dark hair neatly braided. The Little Sisters Fund director mentions that while it wouldn't be unusual for girls their age in the U.S. to talk about growing up to be sports stars or engineers or computer scientists, options are limited in Nepal and it's all too rare for them even to be asked, "What do you want to be when you grow up?" But when the question is put to then now, with the female doctors before them, the girls begin to consider. "Teacher," some say. Many more say "nurse," and there's even a bold girl who declares to much applause that she'd like to be a doctor, and now she has a dynamic pair of role models cheering her on.

On the table in front of the girls are soccer jerseys, a gift carried in by WOGO. Why soccer gear? "Here's the story about the jerseys," Robyn says. "A high school friend reached out to me when she found out we were headed to Kathmandu. She and the other soccer moms in her community in New Jersey had started a nonprofit to provide their children's jerseys—complete teams—to kids in the developing world. Their model had been to ship them, but they were having difficulty getting the jerseys to the intended recipients. She asked if we would hand-deliver to kids in Nepal, and we happily complied. They've sent jerseys with us on every trip so far."

It was the first of many connections WOGO has made with groups who share the desire and means to help. The women have been resourceful in their outreach efforts, much to the good of women and girls everywhere they go.

The team has evolved over the years, losing Ginger Holt and Jennifer Cook, and gaining Kathleen Hogan, who's based in New Hampshire, Amanda Marshall-Rodriguez in Texas, Mychelle Shegog Abrams in the D.C. area, and Antonia Chen in Boston. "I know the typical Op Walk 'model' is different in that different surgeons come and go," Robyn says, "but we decided as a group that it was important to us to carefully vet anyone who might join us, so we invite a potential surgeon to come with us on a trip as a guest so we can operate with her, and we can get to know each other. It's worked out beautifully and we are very close. I am closer to my WOGO sisters than I am to some of my lifelong friends."

WOGO's missions have taken the team not just to Nepal but into Latin America and Africa, and Robyn speaks movingly about what WOGO has seen. "Poverty is very different here in the U.S.," she says. "I don't mean to imply that there are not needy people in our own country, because of course there are, but we have so many safety nets and so much more opportunity. Many of our 'poor' carry a cell phone and most have shelter.

"Immediately before our first trip to Nepal, my family and I visited New York City with good friends who were ministering to the homeless on a bread line. We handed out food, socks, and underwear, and prayer cards to the poorest of our poor. Just a few weeks later, I found myself riding a bus through the streets of Kathmandu. As we rode, I spotted a young girl standing on the steps in front of a building, carefully using her hand to push the fresh rain water off the railing into a small cup so she could drink it because it was clean! Safe drinking water in Nepal is hard to find. I thought back to my day in New York and realized that the guy living under a bridge in Manhattan can get a safe drink of water, but people in much of the world cannot.

"In Kathmandu we saw kids playing 'soccer' with a piece of trash, presumably because they didn't have an actual ball. They were having a blast. Would my own kids be able to be that resourceful if all their worldly goods went away?"

Now WOGO regularly carries not just soccer gear but shoes from a charity called Soles4Souls. "Someone on our team knew of them and reached out before our 2011 Guatemala trip," Robyn explains. "Tiffany Turner came as their representative and helped us with the shoe distribution. She has come with us on every trip since then. The look on the faces of the kids or patients who get new shoes is unbelievable. Many of these people have never had new shoes. Ever. The most memorable shoe distribution was the one we did in the Congo. There is a photo from that event of big old Dikembe Mutombo. He's on his knees putting shoes on a tiny little kid at an orphanage. Life-changing. Shoes just seem to go with what we do—we want people to walk! And it's such an intimate gesture, to put shoes on another's feet. This is why Soles4Souls was such a good fit as our partner. They don't simply deliver a box of shoes, they lay their hands on the person, just like we do."

I hope you'll go to YouTube to see the beautiful video of the trip on their "wogoMission" channel, https://www.youtube.com/user/wogoMission. It opens with one of the team's nurses, Lizette Otero, who is overcome with emotion as she tries to describe the feeling that comes with doing this work. "Sitting in front of a patient when they stand after surgery, they take their first step and they look at you..."—Lizette has to pause as her voice breaks—"and you see *LOVE*. It doesn't matter what color we are, what nation we are from, what gender we are, you just see love. That's what makes the difference every time."

I couldn't help but feel proud of all WOGO did there, even when circumstances intervened to keep them from doing everything they'd hoped to.

## Connecting Computers, Connecting Hearts

As the women of WOGO travel on their missions, they're steadily drawing in people who want to help, a circle that has expanded with time. I've saved my favorite WOGO story for last. It's a perfect example of the way giving becomes contagious as we see the generosity of others and find new depths of it in ourselves.

The story starts in 2011, when Robyn and Jennifer Cook arrived in Antigua, Guatemala, to do the scouting for WOGO's first independent Op Walk mission. Looking for an opportunity to help girls and women in the community, they asked the nurses at the hospital to connect them with a local school, which led them to the Escuela Nacional de Niñas Pedro Betancourt, a girls' school right down the street.

"Jen and I had packed some webcams in our bag, thinking that we would like to get a school there connected with a school in the U.S., broadening the horizons of both the American and the Guatemalan kids," Robyn remembers, but when they took the idea to the school's headmaster, "She looked at us like we had three heads. After discussion with our translator, we realized that they had no internet access at the school. That was one of many lessons we would learn—never apply our First World frame of reference to other places.

"We asked what it would take to get them internet access and learned that it was possible and not expensive. The issue was not the lack of access but having someone to help them all, someone to teach the kids technology. The wheels were spinning then, so Jen and I asked what it would cost to hire a teacher. I don't remember the exact number, but it was somewhere in the ballpark of $300 a month. The surgeons and some other members of our team donated the money to hire them a technology teacher for two years.

"At this point we also realized that their 'computer center' consisted of four newish, donated desktop PC's that were not connected to anything and that nobody even knew how to turn on." WOGO tackled that too. When they got back to the U.S., they found a company that was upgrading its laptops and willing to donate the old ones to the school, and by the time they returned for their mission, Robyn says, "We were armed with laptops, webcams, and hope. We spent the first of our days in Antigua at the school, revamping their playground and bringing sports equipment and other donations, and we got the laptops up and running in anticipation of being there the next day for our shoe distribution, the blessing of the computer lab by the chaplain, and a program that the children had planned for us. We had also planned to do the very first Skype call between the local students and some elementary school kids at a school in North Carolina.

"The night before the planned festivities, a few of us went to the school with the headmaster and some of our tech people to try out the computer equipment. We set up the webcam and made a test call to a family member in the U.S. It worked! When I looked over at the headmaster, who was about my age, she had tears streaming down her face. She had never in her life imagined a video call to another country. Something we all took for granted was life-changing for her."

The next day, the local padre blessed the computers ("We all cringed as he doused them with holy water!" Robyn says) and they were in business. With translators in place on both ends, they powered up their connection and Skyped the classroom in North Carolina. "Somewhere I have photos that were coincidentally taken at almost the exact same moment," Robyn says. "One shows the kids in Antigua crowding around a tiny, old PC, while in the other, the American students sit in their beautiful, modern classroom talking to Guatemala on a large smartboard. Neither class wanted the call to end, and it went on for well over an hour. The holy water must have worked, because the connection miraculously held out!"

The story doesn't end there, though. "One final piece of beauty came out of this," Robyn says. "The kids in North Carolina noticed that the students in the new computer lab were standing at their desks because there weren't any chairs—the school couldn't afford them. So unbeknownst to me, they had a fundraiser, and I came to work one day to find a plastic bag of coins and small bills on my desk with a note that they wanted me to get the money to the kids in Antigua so they could have chairs."

The wave of giving that started with Op Walk's life-changing surgeries gains reach and strength as WOGO seeks more opportunities to serve. "What I have learned is that good multiplies," Robyn says. "We have a few different non-profits, each doing our own thing, but when we get together what we can do increases in an exponential fashion."

Will a little girl inspired by WOGO grow up to be an Operation Walk surgeon some day? Will a child who collected piggy bank change to help someone across the world one day dream up the next Op Walk? Never underestimate the impression that giving can make on the heart—or the life path of a child.

## Operation Walk Denver: An Incubator of Support

Doug Dennis is an Operation Walk legend who has nurtured not only his own Denver chapter but many others across the country. He sprang into action after traveling with us to Managua in 2002 and has been a wellspring of ideas and support for the Op Walk mission ever since. "Wow! My first trip was a life-changing event for me," Doug says. "Seeing the poverty and lack of medical access for so many people shook my heart. It was the best week of my orthopedic life—which happens every Operation Walk trip I have participated in. Within the first forty-eight hours of this mission, there was no doubt in my mind that I needed to start my own chapter of Operation Walk."

So committed was he that when he asked his home hospital to donate supplies to his new team and the powers that be said no, he decided he couldn't stay. He found the reception he was looking for at Porter Adventist Hospital. "Early in my negotiations with the hospital CEO, I shared it would be critical that they support my mission work, and he immediately said, 'No problem. That's who we are,' meaning they were a hospital whose mission was to support mission work. I knew immediately it was wise to move my practice there, which has been a great marriage for Operation Walk Denver. They helped me set up a non-profit foundation and have provided all of our medical supplies."

Doug remembers the way he lay awake night after night during and after his team's first solo mission praying that no patients would develop infections (none did), and he remembers running out of the tubing needed to deliver extra oxygen to a patient after his operation—as well as how his nurses improvised a solution with IV tubes. "We have learned that you need to think on your feet a lot during these missions, and all of my team members relish these challenges," he says. Everyone's the better for having faced them, he's found, both when they return for another mission and when they tend patients at home.

I'm in total agreement with Doug when he says that along with unflappability, the ideal Op Walk team member needs "a heart as big as a bushel basket," and he's found an abundance of those both at his hospital and in the community. Op Walk Denver now takes two trips a year, one in the spring and one in the fall, performing sixty-five to seventy joint replacements each time. On the twenty-seven trips they've taken, they've traveled throughout South and Central America, replacing more than 1,900 hips and knees.

The group's strong fundraising efforts, anchored by their annual Walk of Dreams Gala, have enabled them to extend support to the whole Op Walk network. "As we have prospered," Doug says, "I never forgot the educational and financial help we initially received from Operation Walk Los Angeles. We have tried to return the favor by providing similar assistance to others interested in Operation Walk and have helped develop additional chapters in Boston, Syracuse, North Carolina, and South Carolina."

Beyond this, Doug and the Denver Op Walk chapter are moving step by step toward the more expansive goal of giving doctors at mission destinations the training and resources they need to provide joint replacements to their communities themselves. Through a program called Operation Walk University, Doug says, "we bring healthcare providers from sites we routinely visit to travel to our hospital in Denver to work with my team members and learn more on how to better care for their patients." Occasionally they also pay to bring patients and a family member to Denver, where they can safely do complex surgery that would be too risky to perform at the international site.

One of the most ambitious initiatives his group has in the works is aimed at increasing the supply of affordable implants in the areas they visit. It's always been part of our core mission to introduce total joint replacement, but when implant devices are prohibitively expensive, doctors have little chance to use what they've learned after we leave, and patients continue to be cut off from surgery. Doug calls that "one of the saddest parts of Operation Walk." However, he's got a plan: his foundation is working out ways to purchase implants from local vendors in the countries the Denver group visits, negotiating prices low enough to make them accessible to local surgeons. After this supply chain is established, he says, "we hope our work can indirectly continue through those international healthcare providers we have trained."

That would be a gigantic stride toward my original dream of improving medicine—and improving lives—with Operation Walk.

Behind all this organizing, administrating, and coordinating is one of those bushel-basket sized hearts. Doug's care and compassion are ever-present as he talks about this work we do, always circling back to our patients— what we bring them and what they so freely give us in return. You can hear Doug at his truest as he tells the story of a patient named Maria.

## The Gift of Helping Maria

"Maria came to us from a remote village in the mountains of Panama, where she lived in a home that was supplied with electricity, but used wood fires for heat and cooking. She was twenty-one when we met her and had developed juvenile rheumatoid arthritis as a child. As is typical with the majority of patients we see, she never received the medical treatment she required. Unlike the adult form of rheumatoid arthritis, the juvenile variety results in a great amount of joint stiffening, and some joints may just grow together, with total loss of motion. That's what happened to Maria. As she moved through childhood, her joints became more and more damaged from arthritic inflammation. She had to drop out of school in her teenage years simply because she could no longer get up and climb a flight of stairs to reach her classes. You can imagine what ensued. Maria was lonely and depressed, even to the point of having suicidal thoughts because she felt she was such a burden to her family.

"Her parents had tried to get her to Panama City for our patient clinic, but bus transportation from her village had failed that day. She eventually made it a few days later, though. Our surgery schedule was full by then, but a member of the Panamanian staff stopped me as I was coming out of a knee replacement and told me about her. Would I see her anyway? I said I would, and I'm lucky I did. Being able to care for her has been one of the highlights of my career.

"Ordinarily, I would've received her medical history and X-rays while I was still in Denver, months before the mission, but I could clearly see the extent of her need as she sat before me. Maria was not only in a wheelchair but 'molded' to it. Both of her hips and knees were profoundly stiff and stuck in a flexed position. This is something that I often saw early in my career thirty years ago, when forty percent of the joint replacements I performed were in patients afflicted with advanced rheumatoid arthritis. Over the decades, that number has dropped to five percent because of major advances in medications that can prevent arthritic destruction of the joints, but they were never an option for Maria. One dose of these newer medications costs more than she, and many patients like her, would earn in a year.

"Her X-ray showed severe arthritic destruction of both hips and both knees. The other problem was that her growth had been stunted by her uncontrolled arthritis and she was very small. She weighed only about 100 pounds. I was moved by her pain and determined to help her, but could I do it safely? When dealing with patients like her, if you only perform a single joint replacement, her right hip for example, the stiffness in her other arthritic hip will still limit her movement and keep her from maintaining the flexibility her right side gains with the operation. Therefore, ideally you want to replace both hips at the same time. But Maria's body was so small that the blood loss involved in a bilateral operation would create a greater risk for her than a larger patient. Like most smaller patients, she'd likely require multiple blood transfusions.

"I left her X-rays taped to my hotel window, studying them and trying to decide what was best for her. Finally, I determined that while not ideal, bilateral hip replacements were her best chance. We'd be coming back to Panama in six months for another mission and I could replace both of her knees then.

"I replaced both of her hips, and as expected we needed blood transfusions, but there were no complications. The next day, Maria walked with a walker for the first time in a number of years. Her recovery was smooth, uneventful. Six months later, we replaced both her knees, and today, she walks normally, with no need for a cane or a walker.

"Her story feels like a fairy tale to me," Doug says. "Her severely depressed state is gone, replaced by happiness. She has returned to school, and every time we journey to Panama, she comes and works in our mission to help other Panamanians in need. She is so appreciative. We asked her if she would be willing to come with her mother to Denver to attend our Walk of Dreams Gala, even though before she had been introduced to Operation Walk, she had never even been to Panama City, let alone leaving her country. She agreed to come.

"In Denver, my team members took her and her mother shopping and bought them clothes for the event. No one in the audience at the gala knew of Maria, so one of my Spanish-speaking team members stepped to the stage that night and told her story, then invited her up for an interview. A beaming Maria walked up the stairs normally and brought down the house. She did it again when she revealed that she had brought us a $75 donation that she had collected from people in her village, a fortune from people who have so little. I cried then, and I'm crying again as I remember.

"I wanted for her to keep the money for herself and family, but then remembered the advice of one of my college roommates who went on to be a minister. He always said, 'Don't ever deny someone the gift of giving.' Maria gave us more than she could've known and the attendees at that year's Gala matched her generosity with their own, helping us raise more money for Operation Walk than any fundraising event we'd ever had."

I'm so moved to hear Doug tell Maria's story. Giving begets gratitude begets giving. We see it again and again, in our patients, yes, but also in ourselves. *This* is why we do what we do.

## Operation Walk Canada:
## Treat the Disease, but Prevent It Too

I have always been something of a Johnny Appleseed with Operation Walk, working to spread our work far and wide, but our good friends in Canada, Bob Bourne and Cecil (Cec) Rorabeck, have nurtured Op Walk in a different and very fruitful way. You could say they and Op Walk Canada, based in London, Ontario, are tending Op Walk orchards, and seeing the benefits that come from returning to just a couple of destinations again and again.

Bob, Cec, and their team took their first mission to Antigua, Guatemala in 2006, and Op Walk Canada has returned to Hermano Pedro Hospital ever since, doing sixty-five to seventy-five total joint replacements each time they return. Bob explains what that allows them to do:

"First, we have been able to provide consistent access and ongoing care for a large number of very disabled, economically disadvantaged patients in need of total joint replacement surgery. As our mission has become known, patients have travelled from not only every corner of Guatemala, but also from many surrounding countries to see us," he says. "Second, we have been able to make significant improvements to Hermano Pedro Hospital, which help not only our mission, but also the other forty-seven diverse medical groups who use this facility. Through the generosity of several of our donors, most of whom prefer to remain anonymous, we have been able to install air conditioning in all the operating rooms, upgrade the surgical lighting, provide new anesthesia machines, purchase several sterilization machines and acquire patient monitors for both the surgical and recovery rooms."

They've made an angel of the Canadian government and their ambassador to Guatemala, who by now know Op Walk and the difficulties it faces. "This relationship has been beneficial on many occasions," Bob says, "for example, when our surgical supplies were held up by Guatemala customs or when we were seeking support from Canadian corporations who do business in Guatemala." A long-term relationship with Antigua and the hospital has also helped keep volunteers safe, which is always a top Operation Walk priority. "Guatemala suffers from a history of poverty, inequity, political upheaval, and crime," Bob says. "Knowing the environment in which we are working and establishing ground rules for our volunteers has gone a long way in protecting our team. In addition, our efforts in Guatemala are treasured by the local community, who go out of their way to promote our wellbeing."

The benefits Bob and his team have brought to Antigua are significant, as is another pathway that Operation Walk Canada has followed: giving some of their missions a tight focus on treating a single condition. They took this tack in 2008, after Dr. Tom Greidanus, the founder of a Calgary-based medical mission group called Operation Esperanza, invited Bob and another Canadian doctor, Jim Powell, to join a mission to Cuenca, Ecuador, which Operation Esperanza had been serving for fifteen years.

## A Focus on Young Women, and then on Babies

Both Bob and Dr. Powell were struck by the large number of young adult patients who suffered from the effects of developmental dysplasia of the hip (DDH), which is prevalent there. People with that condition are born with hip sockets too shallow to keep the thigh bone in place, so it's easily dislocated and they suffer debilitating consequences when the bone remains out of joint. In babies and young children, it's easy to treat, guiding the ball of the thigh bone into the hip socket and bracing it there, but in poor countries, the condition often goes undiagnosed and untreated. This is something I've repeatedly noticed as we've operated in Latin America. Some of the most moving cases I've worked on have involved young women suffering from DDH. By the time I see them, they've often developed severe arthritis and may have chronic limps because one leg rides much higher in the hip than the other. These patients always have great pain and stiffness, and often, their bodies have contracted in such a way that their legs scissor over each other, leaving them unable to spread their legs. In addition to having trouble walking, they have great difficulty with sex, and childbirth is impossible without a caesarian, which is too expensive for them to afford.

Astounded by the unmet need for DDH reconstructive surgery, Bob teamed up with Dr. Powell for a joint mission to Cuenca in 2009. Jim Powell later founded his own medical mission focused in part on pediatric orthopedic surgery, and Bob decided to take Operation Walk to Cuenca to treat young adults—the vast majority of them women—with DDH.

"The volume of patients quickly exceeded the capacity of our waiting room and the overflow extended outside the hospital and stretched for more than two city blocks!" Bob remembers. "We were distressed to see so much suffering from DDH hip pathology, a disease which is largely preventable."

Correcting DDH in adults requires complex surgery. The condition leaves small, underdeveloped bones, and many patients need to have their thigh bones shortened to bring their hips down safely from their dislocated positions to where their hip joints were meant to be. Such cases used to be fairly common in North America, accounting for about thirty percent of total hip replacements performed in Canada and the U.S. in the 1970s. "But early detection and treatment programs for DDH have reduced this to less than five percent today," Bob says. "Indeed, if a newborn is diagnosed with DDH at birth and treated for as little as six weeks, the hip is allowed to develop normally and last for a lifetime. Unfortunately, this is not the case in Ecuador, particularly in the Andean highlands, where the prevalence of DDH is among the highest in the world."

So in a fascinating evolution of Op Walk's work, the Canadian team broadened its focus beyond treatment of DDH in Ecuador and launched new initiatives for *prevention*. "It quickly became obvious that we had an important role to play in helping our Ecuadorian colleagues establish an early diagnosis and treatment program for infants with DDH," Bob says. They worked with the country's health authorities to work out a DDH treatment pathway from diagnosis to treatment, then contacted other Canadian and American missions (four doing pediatric surgery and four who work on adults) that have a special interest in DDH and regularly travel to Ecuador. They also partnered with the International Hip Dysplasia Institute, which gave them educational materials in Spanish and baby mannequins for demonstrations. In Ecuador, babies are traditionally bound tightly in swaddling blankets with their legs extended, which puts them at great risk for dysplasia, so trainers show mothers alternate ways to wrap and carry their infants, as well showing them how to examine a baby's hips and if needed, how to use a harness that holds a baby's legs apart and thigh bones in their sockets, an effective, low-tech way to treat newborns with this condition. The educational program gives presentations to healthcare providers in medical schools, hospitals and clinics, and it reaches into small, rural clinics where patients and their family members can learn about DDH.

"The response has been overwhelming," Bob says, "and has led to a 'train the trainer' program which has greatly extended the reach of our program and is beginning to have a real impact in treating DDH early in Ecuador."

## Thinking About the Next Generations

I'm in awe of what all of us have built, what we all aspire to, and what we continue to do. I was already in my mid-fifties when I began Operation Walk, and so were many of the friends who joined me on the early missions, surgeons like Bob Bourne and Merrill Ritter and Doug Dennis, who caught the fever and nurtured the first Op Walk chapters in cities across North America. More than two decades in, I'm encouraged to see us thinking about the future.

I know we have bold young leaders, people like Dr. Victoria Brander in Chicago, who co-founded the team there with one of my "first-generation" friends, Dave Stulberg, and who, like so many of the people who been pulled into this orbit, carries some of the original Operation Walk DNA. Our passionate women of WOGO, our growing Irish team, our inspiring friend Dr. Phuc Vo and the bright lights in our New York chapter and beyond make me confident that the branches of Operation Walk will continue to spread wide, as does every passionate volunteer who joins us and embraces our mission, and every Op Walk veteran who nurtures those who come next.

Bob Bourne talked about succession planning and sustainability when he and Cec Rorabeck handed over the group's medical director roles to Dr. Steve MacDonald and Dr. Jamie Howard, surgeons they know can fill their very large shoes. Summing up the outlook for the next phase of Operation Walk Canada, Bob expressed his faith in Op Walk volunteers, the force that I know will carry Op Walk as a whole into the coming decades.

"Our volunteers are not one and done," he says, "but rather tend to volunteer for one mission after another. Many have volunteered for five, ten, twenty or more missions despite having to raise the money to cover their own mission expenses and to work extremely hard. We are a true team who value the contribution of each volunteer in making each mission a success.

"The willingness of the next generation of volunteers to step forward and continue this good work is heartwarming," he adds. "Our world has many inequities and those of us who have been lucky enough to have been born in wealthy countries are not only fortunate, but have a responsibility to lend a hand up to those less fortunate. Bill Gates perhaps said this best when he stated, "Is the rich world aware of how 4 billion of the 6 billion live? If we were aware, we would want to help out, we would want to get involved."

And we do, in this Op Walk family—all of us, every team, every angel and supporter and every volunteer.

Operation Walk has shaken us awake and shown us what's in our power to do, what we *must* do, and how good that feels.

When I think about how far we've come and the world of need that surrounds us, I think about Olympian Terry Fox, who famously set out to run the width of Canada on a prosthetic leg to raise cancer awareness. "Even if I don't finish," he said, "we need others to continue. It's got to keep going."

There's no stopping us now.

# FINAL REFLECTIONS:

## My Grandfather, My Father,
## and the Crooked Man

...........................................................................

I felt more of a kinship with our Operation Walk patients than they and our hosts ever imagined. I come from people who work the land, and growing up in Iowa, I spent every summer on the Dorr family farms, either my grandfather's or my uncles', where I pulled a lifetime's worth of weeds and labored in the fields alongside my family and paid farmhands from dawn to dusk. If he had been healthy enough, my father probably would have been a farmer himself, and might have raised me as one as well, but he contracted tuberculosis of the spine from drinking infected cow's milk when he was twelve years old, and that changed our trajectory.

TB hit child after child in the 1920s before milk was widely pasteurized, and mostly it infected their bones, not lungs, the way it did in adults. No one knew what was wrong with Dad for a while, but they knew it was bad. My uncles remember how he had abscesses hanging from his back as he guided the horse-drawn plow through the fields, and how my grandma drained them with a spoon. Finally, a chiropractor told my grandfather that Dad had TB, and Grandpa took his entire herd of dairy cows up the gravel road into town and had the vet destroy them all because he wasn't sure which one had the TB-infected milk.

Dad seemed to be at nature's mercy. Fifty percent of the kids who got this TB died from it, the doctors said. The disease progressed, destroying the discs in Dad's back, and his vertebrae collapsed. But Grandpa heard of a new surgery, a spinal fusion, that could make Dad's back steady again.

Grandpa drove him to the Mayo Clinic, and took a chance on the new operation—Dad would be just the fifth person to receive it. He was hospitalized for six weeks, and Grandpa sat by his bed, swearing that if Dad lived, he'd send him to school to become a minister—he promised my father to God. When Dad was stable enough to come home in a body cast, Grandpa put him on a cot and rented a rail car to carry him home, because the tires of a 1920s auto could easily blow on March roads still rutted from winter.

I saw of lot of Grandpa in the families who carried their suffering loved ones and traveled long miles on foot to our clinics. They had the same fear, the same devotion, the same desperate hope. I know Grandpa would've carried Dad to the hospital if he had to, to relieve his pain and try to save him with any new treatment that offered a whisper of a chance.

Sometimes, great leaps come from setbacks and hardships. God works in mysterious ways, as we so often say. It had been a given till Dad's illness that every boy in the Dorr family would stay in school just through eighth grade before going to work full-time on the farm. TB changed that for Dad and sent him to college. It also led him to the love of his life. My mother, Evelyn Knoll, had contracted TB of the hip around the time Dad got sick, and the two of them came in contact when my mom wrote in to a radio show that she was recovering in bed and wanted pen pals. Hundreds of people sent her letters, and she wrote back to Everett Dorr. They kept up their correspondence for eight years, and finally, when both of them were at college, they decided to meet. They married two years later.

So you could say I'm a child of TB, shaped by the way the disease and its aftermath changed my parents' lives. The innovative surgery Grandpa took a chance on saved my father from lifelong disability—it was a miracle. It wasn't "perfect" or thoroughly proven, but that wasn't anyone's measure of what it needed to be. Because of it, Dad was alive and able to move. *That* was the blessing. He wore a back brace and couldn't play sports, but he was endlessly grateful for all that had been restored to him. He became a warrior for the disadvantaged, and the effects of that single operation traveled through our family, our community, through me, and on through the world.

*Do unto others as you'd have them do unto you* was what my father preached and lived. *Give thanks for your many blessings and pass them on.* He and Mom expected me to do the same. Operation Walk has been the culmination of everything they taught me.

I have always been a risk-taker by nature, and my family history was always there reminding me of what medicine can do and how powerfully its advances can reach into our lives and change their course. It made sense to me to innovate and invent for the sake of patients, and to value discovery more than I held onto certainty. I felt and saw the wonder of medicine. I was here on Earth because of it, and I wanted to be part of advances like the surgery my father received. But it took Operation Walk to truly bring science, love, and faith together in me as equals. Op Walk let me see that medical wonders mean the most when they're *received* with a sense of wonder—from patients and families, from doctors and from medical teams—and we feel a kind of awe pass between us—for medicine and our part in it, for the healing we give and receive. We feel gratitude; love fills us up and sends us on with more to give.

In the 1990s when Operation Walk started, experiences like that hardly seemed to exist in my profession anymore. There was less gratitude on all sides, with more mistrust and distance between doctors and patients, more resentment, regulations, and paperwork. Institutions interested in profits seemed to forget the power of a healing personal relationship between doctor and patient, but on Operation Walk, doctors were free simply to serve, and patients and their families were much like my own grandfather and father, experiencing healing they'd hoped for but didn't take for granted. They were amazed and grateful when we treated them, and they gave our work meaning again.

Everyone who's ever gone on an Operation Walk mission has seen and felt the healing it creates and the soul hunger it satisfies. We volunteers know for certain that our work makes a difference.

Personally, I believe God had His hand in this—it is hard to explain another reason why I went ahead with such a crazy idea. Operation Walk happened because I had perseverance, the right people helping me—Jeri especially, Mary Ellen, and Marilyn supporting me all the way—and so many old friends and colleagues willing to take a chance.

Knowing the power of gratitude as I do now, I want to say thank you to them, to my parents and family and mentors, to the patients who changed me, and all who have given so much. Thank you for what all of you have brought to life.

In Operation Walk, we say again and again that while we can't change the entire world, we *can* change the world of every individual we touch. Those words are our core belief and our prayer. We see on each mission how the effect of restoring mobility and dignity to just one person multiplies, lifting whole families and communities, lifting us.

In each patient's face, each miracle of a first step after years of pain, we rediscover our purpose: to give of our talents, our resources, our selves, for the good of others. It's easy to think that our efforts are too small, that we can never do enough, but we keep aiming to help the next person and the next, because just one person is a world, a universe. In that spirit, I would like to leave you with the story of just one man. He's not so different from the thousands of others we've met, but in him I can see the soul of Operation Walk and all we have tried to do over the past twenty-two years.

## The Crooked Man

None of us really knows where the journey of our life will lead us. Philosophers can debate whether it is governed by fate or just unexpected, but it is certain that if you are born in Los Angeles, your journey will be different from that of a young man born in rural Guatemala.

Rogelio Montepeque Estrada lived all of his sixty-two years in the far north of the country near the Mexican border, buffeted relentlessly by circumstances beyond his control. The cruelty of his father drove him from their hardscrabble farm when he was only ten years old. Instead of attending school he went to work washing wood in a factory for one quetzal a day, the equivalent of just a few cents in U.S. money. Work was all he knew through his youth and adult life. He never got any formal education, and even now, he cannot write a sentence because he doesn't know how to spell. Young Rogelio never traveled far from the home his mother made with his six sisters and one brother. Then his mother died, and the family fell further apart.

Rogelio found work as a hired hand in the fields, earning sixty quetzals a day (the equivalent of less than eight dollars) tending crops of corn, beans, and tobacco. He cleared weeds from farmers' land by wielding a machete, working from five thirty in the morning until two in the afternoon, when he would enjoy taking walks with his friends. On weekends, he would drink beer and dance with the ladies. As a laborer, his legs were his strength, his best asset for living a productive and happy life. They carried his self-esteem and his self-image as a man with the ability to work hard. But when he was fifty-seven, his legs began to betray him. As a forty-year-old, even a fifty-year-old, Rogelio could not have guessed that the controlling influence in his life would become his knees. For most of his life he had been a good hired hand in the fields, but as his knees began to ache, the quality of his work began to fall off and his bosses questioned his desire. That bothered Rogelio because he knew how to work. He never slacked off. He had never injured his legs so why was this happening to him?

Who would he be if he became crippled like some he saw in town? He feared what that would mean for him. Crippled meant outcast. He would be damaged goods and no one would give him the work he wanted to do. The greatest possession he had was his worth as a strong worker, and now it was slipping away. Finally, he couldn't carry on. The bosses in the fields let him go.

By the time he was sixty, his knees were bowed so badly his friends joked that he looked like he had been glued together just to ride horses. The physician in his town said there was nothing more that could be done by Guatemalan doctors. He did give Rogelio hope by telling him of American missions that came to the town of Antigua and performed operations. Maybe he could qualify for one of those.

Rogelio begged his friends for the bus fare, 120 quetzals (about $17), for a trip that would carry him six hours from his town to Antigua in the central highlands and six hours back home. He made this journey to Antigua *forty* times, and forty times he was told he could not have the operation because there were too many others in front of him or because no doctor had the required skill to help. Finally a nurse told him there was a new American medical team coming in August, so Rogelio decided to try one more time.

When August came, he boarded the Antigua-bound bus. The two steps he needed to climb were almost impossible for him to negotiate, but the driver offered a hand to pull him inside. He stumbled forward to a free seat and fumbled his crutches onto the overhead rack, then eased himself into a seat on the aisle because he knew he couldn't sit six hours with his knees bent behind the seat in front of him. At least on the aisle he could extend his aching legs.

When they reached Antigua, he struggled out and hobbled on his crutches along the cobblestone streets to Hermano Pedro Hospital. Going inside, he looked down a long hall and saw benches full of people in need like him. Many others were standing. All were waiting to be examined by the local doctor and hoping to be treated by the visiting surgical team. It was late afternoon when a doctor finally saw him, sweeping into the room with his long white coat trailing behind. The doctor put his hand on Rogelio's shoulder. "We cannot do your surgery," the doctor said. "It will take a special implant to straighten your legs, and we don't have it with us. We can tell the next team to bring it." Rogelio nodded his head. He had expected rejection because he had experienced it before, all forty times he'd come. He would go to his sister's house on the outskirts of Guatemala City, and in a few days, he'd return to the mountains.

Mary Ellen Sieben, the only chief operating room nurse Operation Walk has ever had, recognized Rogelio from previous missions. *Maybe this will be the last time he has to wait,* she thought. She held onto his X-rays and the next day, she showed them to me. She knew I wouldn't be daunted by the complexity of his case. I studied the films, then arranged to drive out to Guatemala City with our translator, Pablo, and one of the guests on this mission, Gayle Garner Roski, an artist and philanthropist who had come to chronicle the trip in her paintings.

We found the house where Rogelio's sister lived and sat in the small front room on an L-shaped couch, listening to Rogelio tell his story. At the end of it, I asked Rogelio what he dreamed of doing if he got the surgery. The answer wasn't extravagant. He had no wish to travel to a faraway land or win a pretty lady's hand or become rich. He just wanted to be free of pain and have legs that worked. I told him I could straighten his legs and his pain would be gone. I would do the operation the next day—no need to wait for a special implant or another team.

Rogelio was quiet at first, then he knew it had to be true. He'd been selected. His face spread into a smile and he struggled to stand, a momentous task for his crooked legs. He leaned hard on his crutches, and when he was upright, he let them go and raised his arms in celebration. We went outside to the front gate and shared a fist bump to seal the deal.

There was one remaining obstacle. The hospital charges each patient 5,000 quetzals to be admitted even though Op Walk gives all its care for free. Rogelio did not have 5,000 quetzals (nearly $700). Then they told him it would be 5,000 quetzals for each knee. Rogelio despaired, but when Gayle Garner Roski heard about his situation, she quietly told me that she would cover the cost. This was a man who needed an angel, and she was honored to be his.

The operation was complex because the bone was completely missing from one side of Rogelio's tibia. His femur had collapsed into it, and the ligaments that stabilize the outside of the knee were out of place, with the ligaments inside his knee worn away. Along the walls of a nearby conference room stood surgeons from both the United States and Guatemala, who watched on video as I showed them techniques to correct Rogelio's deformities. The inside of the knee had loose bodies of worn cartilage and debris caused by the rubbing together of the bones. I cleaned up the area and replaced the missing bone by making a graft from Rogelio's own bone, which I'd removed in the process of sculpting the knee bones for the implants. This graft provided a stable scaffold on which I could implant the components of the knee replacement. Then I realigned the ligaments to finish straightening his legs and stabilizing his knees. Rogelio's crooked legs, first one then the other, became straight, and now the U.S. doctors who observed had the techniques they'd need to better help the next Rogelio. There were smiles on the faces of everyone inside the operating room and outside in the halls of the theater.

This is the best of medicine. We had enabled a man who wanted only a good, simple life to have it once more. His crooked legs had taken away his freedom and his livelihood, but the Op Walk team, and his angel, had restored them.

Rogelio was alert soon after his surgery. As the fog in his head cleared he stared at the white ceiling above his bed. There was a crack in it he knew he could repair. He sensed his legs were heavy as lead, and then he knew where he was. He had just had surgery on his knees. The nurses were standing at the end of the bed. Had he lost his legs? He raised his head and instinctively looked down. An involuntary laugh was his first sound, and then tears rolled down his cheeks as he saw what we had done.

It became like Christmas in the recovery room. Rogelio's sister came in, and as soon as she saw his legs she began to sob. The recovery room nurses clapped and cheered, and other nurses and doctors in the area peered in through the hallway door to see what the celebration was all about. They joined in the applause. Gayle smiled widely as she raised her camera to memorialize this success. Soon a Facebook notice would go out, an announcement to the world of one more small Op Walk miracle.

The Crooked Man was straight.

## THE END
................

# Operation Walk's Teams and Leaders

......................................................................

We began the great Operation Walk experiment with a small team from Los Angeles, and we've grown to twenty groups today. Here's our history at a glance, along with the names of some of the key people who've believed in our grand idea—and run with it.

- **1997: Los Angeles.** Dr. Larry Dorr, founder and lead surgeon. Jeri Ward, RN, Mary Ellen Sieben, RN, team leaders.

- **2000: Indiana**. Dr. Merrill Ritter, founding lead surgeon. Dawana Page, team leader.

- **2003:** Denver. Dr. Douglas Dennis, founding lead surgeon. Peggy Kettler, RN, Jim Boyle, PA, team leaders.

- **2005: Boston.** Dr. Thomas Thornhill, founding lead surgeon. Roya Ghazinouri, PT, team leader.

- **2005**: **Chicago.** Dr. David Stulberg, Dr. Victora Brander, founding lead surgeons. Jane Guzman, Sophie Sauser, Odell Woods, team leaders.

- **2006**: **Virginia.** Dr. Gerald Engh, founding lead surgeon. Laura McCormack, RN, Connie Roof Kohler, OT, Tracy Woodward, RN, team leaders.

- **2006: London, Ontario, Canada.** Dr. Cec Rorabeck, Dr. Bob Bourne, founding lead surgeons. Anna Hales, RN, Tracy Rau, RN, team leaders.

- **2008: Maryland**. Dr. Paul Khanuja, founding lead surgeon. Dotsie Czajkowski, ONP, Maria Khanuja, CRNP, team leaders.

- **2009: Pittsburgh.** Dr. Anthony M. DiGioia, founding lead surgeon. Angela DeVanney, Sandra Nettrour, RN, team leaders.

- **2009: Utah.** Dr. Aaron Hofmann, founding lead surgeon. Cathy Groos, Sylvia Sorenson, team leaders.

- **2010: WOGO.** Dr. Jennifer Cook, Dr. Robyn Hakanson, Dr. Ginger Holt, Dr. Rinelda Horton, Dr. Audrey Tsao, founding lead surgeons. Michelle Burdette, RN, Shawn Tylka, Pia Rena, RN, team leaders.

- **2011: Syracuse.** Dr. Brett Greenky, Dr. Seth Greenky, founding lead surgeons. Kimberly Murray, RN, team leader.

- **2012: Manitoba, Canada.** Dr. David Hedden, founding lead surgeon. Sharon Irwin, RN, Claudio Videtto, team leaders.

- **2013: Oregon (Freedom to Move).** Dr. Paul Duwelius, founding lead surgeon. Beverly Haynes, Vicki Warneking, team leaders.

- **2016: South Carolina/Nicaragua (Walk Nicaragua).** Dr. H. Del Schutte, founding lead surgeon. Jacklyn Rinaldi, RN, Sarah Voges, FNP-C, team leaders.

- **2016: Ireland.** Dr. Derek Bennett, Dr. David Cogley, founding lead surgeons. Claire Keating, RN, Grainne Duffy, RN, Niamh Laffey Flynn, RN, team leaders.

- **2017: North Carolina.** Dr. Bryan Springer, founding lead surgeon. Kristi Sylvester, RN, Paul Coleman, PA, team leaders.

- **2017: Idaho.** Dr. Keith Holley, Dr. Jared Armstrong, founding lead surgeons. Nicole Pyle, PA-C, Pat Armstrong, team leaders.

- **2018: Florida.** Dr. Keith Gustke, Dr. Phuc Vo, Dr. Brian Palumbo, founding lead surgeons. David Giles, team leader.

- **2019: Albany, NY.** Dr. Jared Roberts, founding lead surgeon. Kelly Roberts, Megan Cody, RN, Rachel Stoner, RN, team leaders.

Please note: It takes a very large village to make Operation Walk run, and we apologize to those we have omitted from these lists. We value the efforts of everyone who has contributed to our work and we hope you will accept our thanks.

# The Donors and Sponsors
## Who've Made Everything Possible

..................................................

It's expensive to take Operation Walk Los Angeles around the world. Op Walk provides air travel, housing, and meals for its volunteer team members, and while many of its supplies are donated, the group covers the cost of any that are not.

Our generous donors enable us to do this. We appreciate all the friends, colleagues and former patients who have made contributions, and owe a debt of gratitude to the team members who have donated their own airfare. We would like to give special thanks to those listed below, whose gifts of time, skills, wisdom, and money have enabled us to grow and thrive. We are forever grateful for their belief in Operation Walk and for their support through the years. They have allowed us to give the gift of mobility, and change thousands of lives.

- Ana Senior
- Anita P. Yagjian
- Bea and Paul Bennett
- Brent N. Burns
- Carl West
- Charles D. and Carolyn Miller
- David and Melissa Hotchkin
- Dr. Benjamin and Annabelle Bierbaum

- Dr. Nicholaas Budhiparama
- Dr. Dang-Khoa Vo
- Dr. Dickey and Susan Jones
- Dr. John and Shelley Kumar
- Dr. Jonathan and Rocki Cohen
- Dr. Lawrence and Marilyn Dorr
- Dr. Paul and Cindy Gilbert
- Dr. William T. Long
- Ed and Gayle Garner Roski
- Ed and Kate Woodsome
- Esther E. Carey
- Gaspar and Cindy Porcell
- Jane Lyon
- Jay A. Cohen
- Jean E. Hide-Cohen
- Jeffrey and Allison Mirkin
- Jeri and Greg Ward
- Jill and Bob Baffert
- John and Kim Callaghan
- Linda and John Seiter
- Lisa and George Etheridge Jr.
- Lori Evensen
- Majestic Realty Co.
- Myna and Uri Herscher
- Paula E. Paulus
- Reon Roski
- Rich and Kathy Cadarette

- Richard and Kathy Link
- Richard J. Hirrel
- Robert and Kathy Goodwin
- Sheva Carr
- Steven and Denise Botsford
- Suzanne Searle Dixon Trust
- USC Verdugo Hills Hospital LLC
- William Harris

# Sponsors

The following companies have supplied Operation Walk Los Angeles with annual donations of many of the items we need to accomplish an Operation Walk mission—everything from implants to Band-Aids. We are grateful for their generous support. Our work would be impossible without them.

- AmeriCares
- Cardinal Health
- Centinela Hospital Medical Center
- CHA Hollywood Presbyterian Medical Center
- Direct Relief
- Good Samaritan Hospital
- Huntington Hospital
- Keck School of Medicine of USC
- Medline
- Steris
- Stryker
- SunMedica
- The Remedy Pharmacy, Torrance, CA
- Total Joint Orthopedics
- USC Verdugo Hills Hospital
- Zimmer Biomet

We would also like to give our deep thanks to Margaret Leslie Davis, who helped immeasurably with the production of this book.

OPERATION WALK

www.operationwalk.org